STOP SMILING
START KVETCHING

A 5-Step Guide to
Creative Complaining

BARBARA HELD, PH.D.

Audenreed Press
A Division of Biddle Publishing Company

This book is not intended to take the place of professional therapy.

Publisher's Cataloging-in-Publication Data

    1. Held, Barbara S.
    2. Stop Smiling, Start Kvetching:
       A 5-Step Guide to Creative Complaining
    3. Self-Help
    4. Humor
    5. Social Critique

Library of Congress Catalog Card Number: 98-74103

ISBN 1-879418-69-X

Grateful acknowledgment is made for permission to reprint the following cartoons:

> Cartoons by Charles Addams, Leo Cullum, Robert Mankoff, and Warren Miller reprinted by permission of cartoonbank.com.

> "Highway Scene" reprinted by permission of Amy Hill (amyhill.com) and KABOOM!, New York City.

> PEANUTS reprinted by permission of United Feature Syndicate, Inc.

Audenreed Press/A Division of Biddle Publishing Company
PMB 103, P.O. Box 1305
Brunswick, Maine 04011
(207) 833-5016
www.biddle-audenreed.com

Dedicated to the memory of Aldo Llorente, M.D.

ACKNOWLEDGMENTS

A great many people have helped me refine my kvetching technique over the years. My thanks to them—some of them know who they are—and to the following friends, colleagues and family, who gave, in addition, their encouragement and advice: Charles Beitz, David Bellows, Chandler Bellows, Gus Bellows, Michael Boyd, Barbara Weiden Boyd, James Coyne, Barry Duncan, Gert Eisenlob, Don Gallant, Harriette Held, Milton Held, Roberta Held, Cynthia Koch, Arnold Lazarus, Mary Lefkowitz, Lisa Levinthal, Sir Hugh Lloyd-Jones, Nancy Love, Suzanne Lovett, Al Mahrer, Lou Marinoff, Antonia Rachiele, Karen Robbins, Paul Schaffner, George Schmiedeshoff, Donna Trout, Peter Trumper, Marilynn Vander Schaaf, Eliot Werner, Lewis Zager, and Julie Zimmerman.

"I feel we've had a good session today."

CONTENTS

PREFACE

I've had the usual assortment of problems in my life—relationship problems, physical problems, emotional problems, you name it. (The current problem involves two injured ankles—two injured Achilles tendons, if you really want to know. More about that particular problem later. But here let me say that my ankles are killing me.) When I have a problem, I try to solve it by doing many reasonable things:

- I seek good advice from people whose opinions I trust. Sometimes I even follow that advice.

- I occasionally get therapy—not too often, though, for reasons I will explain.

- I try to distract myself with work, socializing, reading, music, movies, and exercise (which I can't do now because of my two injured Achilles tendons).

In short, I use the usual coping methods.

While each of these methods has its good points, none

of them works as well for me as kvetching. I'm a born kvetcher, and nothing helps me cope with life as well as kvetching. In fact, I've been told that I started kvetching as soon as I could talk, and I know I haven't stopped since. Why should I? It works for me, and if you learn to kvetch correctly, it can work for you too.

In this little book, I share this method of coping. In Part I, I explain what kvetching is, and why it can be a good way to cope with life's difficulties. I also tell you what gets in the way of productive kvetching. In Part II, I discuss the most productive and least productive ways to kvetch to others about your problems. And there I present my 5-Step Guide to Creative Kvetching. In Part III, you will read about famous creative and noncreative kvetchers.

Since I am a psychologist, I base some of my views about kvetching on my therapy practice and on psychological research. But since I'm also a native New Yorker, I base most of my views on my own life experiences. My views are based especially on my own "career" as a kvetcher, and as someone who has taught others how to kvetch. But before we discuss my views, we need to define our terms.

PART I

KEYS TO KVETCHING

CHAPTER 1

BASIC KVETCHING

A few years ago my friend Fred (not his real name) came over for a visit. As soon as he arrived, I could see that he was very upset. So I asked him what was wrong. Without any more prodding, a flood of problems poured out of him.

"My girlfriend dumped me last week, my car needs five hundred dollars' worth of repairs, I just had another fight with my mother about our last visit, and my boss is being a jerk. Other than that, things are *just fine*." The "just fine" was the tipoff. Fred never says that unless things are *not* fine at all.

I responded briefly. "Things sound pretty awful. What can I do to help?"

"Aren't you going to say what everyone else said about my problems?"

"What is that, Fred?" Already I had my suspicions.

"That I should cheer up. That things will get better. That I'm young and will find a new girlfriend. That I'm lucky to be able to afford the five-hundred-dollar repair job. That everyone fights with their mother. That everyone hates their boss or their job or both. Some of my friends even started to tell me how *their* problems are much worse than mine, so what am I complaining about? All this 'help' is making me feel even worse."

My suspicions were confirmed. Fred not only had real problems, but all his well-meaning friends *were* making him feel worse. Their *intentions* were good, but their advice was all wrong. After talking to his friends, Fred still had his original problems, but now he felt even worse for feeling bad about such "minor" matters. He felt bad about not being able to just "cheer up." This made perfect sense to me, and I told Fred as much.

"You know, Fred, your friends are well-meaning, but they just don't get it: You're too upset to just cheer up. And now, after getting all this so-called advice, you feel more upset because you have two sets of problems: Your original problems, and the fact that you can't just take them in stride and 'feel better.' Am I right?"

"I guess so." Fred was still pretty demoralized. He needed hope.

"Listen, have I got a solution for you. It won't fix all your problems, but it will help you feel a little less bad about them. It's called kvetching."

"What's kavetching?" Fred had obviously not heard the word before; he looked skeptical. I could see I had my work cut out for me.

"Not kavetching—kvetching!" Let me explain.

WHY KVETCH?

Kvetching is a method of coping. It usually won't solve all your problems on its own. Nothing, not even good psychotherapy or winning the lottery, can do that. Still, kvetching can help you deal with your problems, bear them, and survive them. The main purpose of kvetching is to unburden yourself. Most people have had the experience of telling their problems to someone else and having a sense of relief afterward. You probably have said to yourself or heard someone else say, "You know, it's good to get that off my chest!" If you have, you know the feeling of relief that kvetching can bring.

But kvetching doesn't always work this way. Sometimes people don't want to listen to your problems. Sometimes they respond to you in ways that make you feel worse. That's what happened to my friend Fred. So it's important to learn to kvetch correctly. By "kvetch correctly" I mean learning to kvetch in ways that do give you that sense of relief, that feeling of having unburdened yourself. In fact, when done correctly, kvetching can also help you relate better to the people you kvetch to. This book is designed to teach you how to kvetch correctly.

Right now, you need to know how to pronounce the

word "kvetch." And you need to know what it means. Then we'll get back to how kvetching can help you cope with your problems.

WHAT IS KVETCHING?

The word "kvetch" is Yiddish. Like the words of any language, there's a right way and a wrong way to pronounce it. "Kavetch" is the wrong way to say it, because this separates the "k" and the "v" sounds too much and so turns what is supposed to be a one-syllable word into two syllables. To say the word "kvetch" correctly, put the "k" and the "v" together, so that the "v" sound follows immediately after you start to say the "k" sound. Then you get the correctly pronounced one-syllable word, which rhymes with the word "stretch."

I begin by kvetching about the correct pronunciation of the word "kvetch" for a serious reason: I have found that people who say the word "kvetch" incorrectly usually don't know how to kvetch. In fact, these are often the same people who have the hardest time learning how to kvetch, even when they *want* to learn. I'm not sure why this is so, but I've got some ideas (see Chapter 3). In any case, it makes sense to begin our kvetching lessons with learning how to pronounce this difficult word. Then you won't have the wrong pronunciation get in your way. In fact, it might be a good idea to take a few minutes now and say the word "kvetch" correctly ten or twenty times out loud. If nothing else, this should serve as a good warming-up exercise. If you already know the correct pronunciation, you can kvetch about how I'm wasting your time with all this nonsense about pronunciation.

Now that we've worked on pronunciation, let's talk about the correct way to use the word "kvetch."

There are two basic ways to use the word "kvetch." First, it can be used to describe a kind of action or activity. For example, "I like to KVETCH," or "KVETCHING is fun for me." Second, it can be used to describe a kind of person. For example, "I am a KVETCHER." Like many Yiddish words, the word "kvetch" is not easy to translate into English. It comes close to each of the following words, but it's not exactly the same as any one of them:

- to complain
- to gripe
- to vent
- to whine
- to bellyache

None of these words quite captures the full meaning of the word "kvetch." Even the full list doesn't do justice to that word. Actually, the word "kvetch" needs many sentences to describe it. Here are three key features of kvetching. Each of the three features needs quite a bit of explanation to make the concept of kvetching clearer.

- **Kvetching Is Persistent**

The kvetcher must complain for some period of time or complain repeatedly. For example, you can't say just once, "I'm not happy," and have it count as real kvetching. To be a kvetcher, you need to say something like this: "You know, I'm not too happy these days. In fact, I've been feeling kind of miserable for some time now. My job's not bad, although I can't stand my boss. My marriage is okay, although my husband gets on my nerves now and then. I don't look forward to life much, but then again I never did. But don't worry about me— all this is nothing new."

- **Kvetching Is Insistent**

The kvetcher insists that the listener pay attention to the kvetcher's kvetching. The kvetcher may even expect the listener to commiserate or agree with the kvetcher's unhappiness. This feature of kvetching is potentially dangerous: It could cause relationship difficulties. Many listeners don't have the patience to hang in there for the duration of prolonged kvetching—after all, they have problems of their own. They might even want to kvetch about their own problems. Later in this book I will discuss this potential drawback to kvetching and make suggestions about how to avoid the negative consequences of kvetching.

• **Kvetching Appears Resigned and Passive**

The kvetcher usually indicates that the problem is beyond the kvetcher's control. Consider the example of kvetching I gave in the section entitled "Kvetching Is Persistent": It should give you the feeling that the particular kvetcher I described there has no intention of changing her situation. You probably even got the sense that she sees no way to fix things. It's safe to say that, in general, kvetchers seem unwilling or unable to take any action—to *do* something to solve their problems.

This third feature of kvetching, like the second feature, is also potentially dangerous. In fact, research has shown that listeners lose patience with people who complain persistently and insistently, but who take no action to make things better. This loss of patience is especially likely when someone complains about matters that seem trivial or minor to the listener. Later in this book, I'll discuss how to avoid the negative consequences that can arise from this third feature of kvetching. I'll also explain how kvetching doesn't automatically prevent taking action. In fact, I'll show how kvetching can actually help you take action.

As you can see, there is no easy way to define the word "kvetch." The easiest way to put it is this: Kvetching is a particular way of expressing dissatisfaction with your circumstances in life, and it contains the three features I just described. There is a fourth feature of kvetching that is so important that I must add it at this point. Actually, it is more of a *non*feature than a feature, because it's a description of what kvetching is *not*:

- **Kvetching Is Not Criticizing the Listener**

The kvetcher must never "kvetch" *about* the person he is kvetching *to*. Not ever! I put the word "kvetching" in the last sentence in quotation marks to make the point that doing this is not even kvetching. It's *criticizing* your listener. Criticizing your listener is completely different from kvetching, and so I will not even discuss how to criticize productively in this book. There are lots of assertiveness-training books that can help you learn to confront and criticize others better.

Of course, you can kvetch to your listener about someone *else*. Then you are criticizing *someone*, but not your *listener*. So kvetching doesn't prohibit criticizing of any sort, just criticizing your listener. Of course, there's danger in kvetching *to* one person (let's call her Alice) *about* another (let's call him Bob): Alice may then kvetch to Bob about your kvetching about him. Bob may then be unwilling to listen to your kvetching about anything or anyone in the future. Life is risky.

WHAT TO KVETCH ABOUT

Now that we have considered what kvetching is and is not, a question arises: What problems or situations in life should you kvetch about? Is kvetching about some situations more appropriate than kvetching about others?

The answer to this question is simple: Aside from criticizing your listener (which is not kvetching), nothing is off limits. Any situation in life that causes you any amount of difficulty or pain is good kvetching material. Having said that, I should tell you that kvetching about trivial or minor matters is probably the most typical form of kvetching. The word "kvetch" has this sort of meaning in Yiddish. My listing of the word "gripe" to translate the word "kvetch" into English may give you the feeling that the kvetcher's problem is always a minor one. Leo Rosten, in his famous book *The Joys of Yiddish*, defines a kvetcher as "A 'sad sack' who magnifies minor aches and pains." But there's no reason to put major aches and pains off limits to the kvetcher. I believe you can kvetch about major matters as well as minor ones. In fact, I think it's even more important to kvetch when life gets really tough. That's when you need kvetching the most.

Still, many people make the mistake of thinking they should ignore the difficulties of life, both large and small. "Why make mountains out of molehills?" they say. I have heard this said about problems ranging from getting a paper cut, to getting news of a serious illness. People also say things like, "Look on the bright side," "Get a positive attitude," "Keep your chin up," and "Cheer up, things could be worse." We've all heard these so-called words of wisdom. The problem is, they either make no sense when you consider life's many hardships, or they actually make matters worse. Remember my friend Fred.

Take the last suggestion in my list just above, that we should "cheer up because things could be worse." The last part of that bit of "wisdom" is true. But this is no cause for cheer. Quite the opposite, this is exactly why we have the right to kvetch, no matter how major or minor the problem may seem at the moment. After all, how many of us have crystal balls? How many of us know for sure that things won't actually get worse? How many of us know that the paper cut won't turn into gangrene? (And who, by the way, gets to decide for each of us which problem is major and which is minor?) In Chapter 2, I tell you more about my philosophy of life. This philosophy justifies our need and our right to kvetch about all problems, great and small.

CREATIVE KVETCHING VS. NONCREATIVE KVETCHING

So where does all this leave us? You now have some idea of what the word "kvetch" means, even though it has no simple English translation. I have also claimed that no problem is too large or too small to kvetch about. You'd think we would have clear sailing on the sea of kvetching from here, right? Wrong!

A problem remains, and it is a serious one: There is always the danger of annoying others because of our kvetching. And if we annoy others enough, we may drive them away. Alienating someone is not a problem if you want that particular person out of your life. (Although let me be clear: I'm not recommending kvetching as the best way to accomplish that goal.) But I have seen people run for cover at the sight of certain kvetchers. As much as I hate to admit it, I myself have been guilty of poor kvetching form at times, even when kvetching about my injured Achilles tendons! So given the difficulty of defining the word "kvetch," and given its potential to create negative reactions in others, a question must be asked: Why would anyone want to promote kvetching as a coping mechanism at all, let alone a good one?

The answer is, because it is a good coping mechanism— good for minor problems and major problems alike. But it's good only if it is done productively, correctly, or with good

25

form. I call kvetching that is done productively, correctly, or with good form "creative kvetching." I call kvetching that is done incorrectly or with bad form "noncreative kvetching." Creative kvetching draws people in; it engages the listener, so you can unburden yourself while improving your relationships. A win-win situation! Noncreative kvetching does just the opposite. It drives people away; it annoys and alienates them. You don't get to unburden yourself, and you may lose friends as well. I end Part I by explaining the obstacles to creative kvetching that most of us face. In Part II, I present my 5-Step Guide to Creative Kvetching. You can think of Part II as a guide to kvetching etiquette: It will help you learn to kvetch without driving people away. As Miss Manners tells us in her etiquette books, the point of all etiquette is to make life go more smoothly, to make *relationships* go more smoothly.

Because I'm a born kvetcher, I have spent a great many years kvetching both creatively and, yes, at times, noncreatively. And because I'm also a psychologist, I have spent lots of time observing and thinking about the difference between the two types of kvetching. I have also spent time thinking about how people can be encouraged to kvetch, and kvetch more creatively at that.

Before turning to my Guide to Creative Kvetching, you need to understand why kvetching should be seen in a positive light when it comes to coping with life's many difficulties. To understand this, you must first understand my philosophy of life. In Chapter 2, I discuss just that.

CHAPTER 2

WHY WE NEED TO KVETCH, OR, MY PHILOSOPHY OF LIFE

Every year I see Bryce, our family doctor, for my annual checkup. Of course, that includes the usual "female" part of the examination. During my examination this year, I told Bryce that I had a plan for the future.

"You know, Bryce, I've been thinking. This being a female business is for the birds. I have a plan."

"What plan now, Barbara?" Bryce always listens to my latest scheme with some blend of curiosity, amusement, skepticism, and sometimes, though he would never admit it, the slightest touch of nervousness.

"You know I don't believe in life after death, reincarnation, and all that spiritual stuff."

"Me too." Bryce is, next to me, the most hard-core realist I know.

"But if we do get reincarnated, and I have any say in the matter, then when I die I'm not coming back as a female.

I'm coming back as a male."

Bryce didn't miss a beat. "Actually, Barbara, why take chances?"

"What do you mean?"

"I mean, why take chances? I'm coming back as a rock!"

Bryce was on to something. After all, being a boy may have its advantages, but it's no guarantee for a disaster-free life either. Better to be an inanimate object, like a rock. Rocks stand a better chance against the elements.

This brings me to my philosophy of life: LIFE IS HARD—ALWAYS! Consider this: Even if life *appears* to being going well in any one moment, what guarantees that it won't change for the worse in the next moment? And if life's not going so well? Or if it's going downright horribly? What's to prevent it from getting even *more* horrible?

Consider my injured Achilles tendons. I tore both of them. This in itself was no easy accomplishment. I didn't need surgery, which was a good thing—I suppose. But I was in for a good year of painful physical therapy. Athletes, of course, do this all the time, but at least they're young. (Oops, competitive kvetching. My mistake. See Step 4, Chapter 7.) I take that back, it's lousy for athletes too. After all, they need to do more than walk on those tendons. Anyway, a few months into my physical therapy, I stretched too hard, and was back to ground zero: I reinjured my tendons. Then I got the flu. Then, to top things off, I had a big falling out with a friend. Remember, the problem is this: Things really *can* always get worse. There are no guarantees in life. That's what makes it so hard. That's why I hate life.

Or consider my friend Fred. His girlfriend dumped him. His car needed five hundred dollars in repairs. He just had another fight with his mother. And his boss was giving him a hard time. You would think he'd be in for a little good luck—statistically speaking, that is. But instead he injured his shoulder. This made it hard for him to swim. Swimming is how Fred copes with stress.

And these are minor problems, compared with what the fates can dish out to us at any time. I'm not even thinking about the horrors of war, famine, plague . . .

KVETCHING AND PSYCHOLOGICAL SCIENCE

Before I give you my philosophy of life, let's see where psychologists stand on the kvetching question. This is a little hard to do, since psychologists don't study kvetching itself. But their work on optimism and complaining is relevant, so that will have to do. And don't worry—no tedious lecture here. Just a quick course to give a nod to science.

Many therapists say optimism is the way to live. And in all fairness, they've got a point. In his best-selling book *Learned Optimism,* psychologist Martin Seligman claims that people can make a shift from a pessimistic to an optimistic attitude, and that this shift can improve their health, mood, and achievements. Dr. Seligman supplies scientific evidence to support his claim, but even he says we shouldn't be slaves to the "tyrannies of optimism." In any case, my goal is not to argue with his evidence: If you want to learn to be more optimistic, I wish you well. But that's not for me. I myself prefer to stick with kvetching. This book is for people like me, people who don't want to put their money on optimism. And this book is also for people who prefer optimism, but who find there are times when optimism just doesn't work for them.

Optimists might be surprised to learn that some research actually supports the benefits of complaining. Psychologists Robin Kowalski and James Pennebaker say that complaining helps you feel better by allowing you to vent your frustrations. In his book *Opening Up*, Dr. Pennebaker showed that when people can express the emotions and facts of a traumatic event, they have fewer health complaints. In fact, they seem to have fewer problems in general. In her book *Aversive Interpersonal Behaviors,* Dr. Kowalski, who also discusses the negative consequences of complaining, says that, among other things, complaining can help you save face by giving you an excuse for a poor performance. I know that's true from personal experience. When I gave a talk about kvetching to answer the question "How Do Therapists Cope with Their Own Personal Problems?," I told the audience that my presentation would have gone much better if my injured Achilles tendons weren't hurting so much.

And you should know that there is controversy within

psychology over an idea called depressive realism. Many psychologists think that depression is caused by an overly pessimistic, distorted view of reality. Psychologists who write about depressive realism say the opposite. They say that depression may be caused by an all-too-accurate take on reality. In fact, depressed people are said to be *too* realistic. It's the rest of us, those of us who are *not* depressed, who may be in a chronic state of denial about just how bad things really are! So an optimistic attitude may have some denial built into it. In any case, I have no objection to an optimistic life strategy, if it appeals to you. I just don't think optimism works for everyone—it certainly doesn't work for me.

MY PHILOSOPHY OF LIFE

My philosophy of life is simple: It's bad enough to face the harsh reality that life is hard—for everyone. But then to be told by therapists, authors of self-help books, "inspirational" speakers, well-meaning (and not so well-meaning) friends, and countless others that we have to act—or worse yet *be*—happy about that fact is to add insult to injury. This demand for that positive attitude—for that optimistic outlook—adds an extra burden to an already heavy load. So life is hard, and then we have to act happy. We have to pretend life is fine when it isn't. We have to appear optimistic when we aren't. "Smile when you're upset," they all tell us. "Celebrate life," they say. "Don't worry, be happy," the

DEPRESSIVE REALISM

Reprinted by permission of
Amy Hill (amyhill.com) and KABOOM!, New York City.

famous song goes.

So it's not being upset itself that's the problem. The real problem is the added pressure of having to deny that life is as hard as it is. The pressure of having to act as if we're not having a hard time when we are. The pressure of having to pretend we're okay when we're really not. All that denying, acting, and pretending takes energy, lots of energy, because it's a pretense. And the pretense keeps us from seeing life as it really is, which presents its own problems.

I once knew a professional woman, Andrea, who objected strongly to my philosophy of life. It made her very upset. Needless to say, she was the most positive person I'd ever met. Her attitude was so positive that she scared me to death: She never griped about *anything*. Not ever. Andrea based her positive outlook on some form of spirituality. But she acted no differently from the way anyone acts when they advocate the power of positive thinking. She lectured me regularly about my "negative attitude" toward life—how wrong I was, how I myself caused my problems with my bad attitude, and so on. She especially objected to my usual response to the typical American greeting, "How are you?," which is, "I hate life" or "I hate everything" (depending on my mood). Andrea thought this reply was nothing less than blasphemy.

And then it happened. Life dealt her a blow she couldn't cope with in her usual way. Andrea lost her job. Then she got sick with a stress-related illness. (Although I'm happy

I HATE EVERYTHING

PEANUTS reprinted by permission of United Feature Syndicate, Inc.

to say, she recovered from the illness and found another job.) But on the worst day of her life Andrea said this to me:

"You know, Barbara, I hate to admit it, but you may be on to something. I think I may hate life too." The tentative "think" and "may" were definitely in there, giving Andrea a bit of an out. But she said the dreaded words nonetheless. So I tried to be a good sport (this wasn't easy). I congratulated Andrea heartily for overcoming her positive attitude.

To make a long story short, the next day Andrea regained her composure. She tried to take back her concession. "It was just a moment of weakness," she said sheepishly.

"Perhaps," I said with a smile. "But once you admit that life is hell, once you say it out loud—well, you just can't take it back. You've got a lifetime membership in my 'I Hate Life' club, whether you want it or not."

Andrea did not look pleased, but she didn't look displeased either. She could certainly return to her old positive attitude, but now she could also kvetch anytime she felt like it. I call that liberation. Of course, we must remember that we can never be fully liberated from that huge difficulty known as life.

For me the road to liberation has been to stop smiling and start kvetching. To be sure, kvetching is not the same as taking action to change the world—although social activists (like most college professors) tend to be pretty good kvetchers. But kvetching can help you see the problems of life more realistically, because it gives you the freedom to stop smiling, to stop pretending the problems aren't there. Then you may decide to do something more about these problems than to deny them with unwarranted optimism, on the one hand, or to kvetch about them, on the other hand. Then again, you may decide that kvetching about them is all you can do, or all you want to do. The choice is yours to make. Remember, kvetching may be a justified end in itself.

Whatever I choose—to kvetch and take action, or to kvetch and let it go at that—the most important thing I've learned so far is this: Facing the reality that life is hard isn't our real problem. If the idea behind depressive realism is right, facing the harsh realities of life can be demoralizing. No doubt about it. But it can also be liberating. Knowing that life is hard for everyone is liberating. Just think what would happen if everyone stopped pretending and admitted they were having a tough time with whatever life was dishing out for them. Then those of us who have a hard time pretending to be okay when we're not would feel less defective. We might even feel more normal. We might, in the words of a kvetchy comedian, finally get some respect!

Of course, there's danger here. If everyone starts kvetching, who will do the listening? What if we become a nation of "Competitive Kvetchers" (see Chapter 7)? Given our two American commandments—"Thou shalt be optimistic" and "Thou shalt have a positive attitude"—I don't think there's any real danger of all Americans becoming kvetchers.

But what if my suggestions are taken seriously? What if I have sown the seeds of a kvetching revolution? Unlikely. Remember, I'm not optimistic. But if I'm wrong about this, my Guide to Creative Kvetching could become especially useful. Fortunately, you don't need to be a part of any revolution to put kvetching to creative good use.

THE LIMITS OF KVETCHING

Let's be honest. There is no body of scientific evidence on which my call for kvetching is based. After all, who's done research on *kvetching*? As I've said, this book is based mostly on my personal experience as a kvetcher. I also like to think it's based on common sense.

Here I want to tell you what kvetching will not do for you, so you don't expect too much. Jackie Kennedy Onassis, who had lots of wealth but also lots to kvetch about, and who was not a kvetcher of any sort (and who was revered by most Americans for her positive attitude), reportedly said that it's best not to expect too much from life. Whether you agree with her or not, it's best to know what kvetching— even creative kvetching—will not do for you. Then your expectations can be realistic.

I stress the importance of realistic expectations because so many self-help gurus promise great things, from material fortune to unbounded personal growth. I make none of these claims for kvetching. My claims are much more modest, because I believe that no amount of self-help, or even professional help, can overcome the fact that life is hard. So it's best to know the limits of kvetching at the start:

- Kvetching will not turn your life into a problem-free utopia.

- Kvetching will not make you a more virtuous, self-actualized, healthy, fulfilled, loved, joyful, intelligent, empowered, centered, complete, wealthy, successful, thin, (you fill in the blank) human being.

- Kvetching will not help you find and save your "inner child" (or your marriage), or put you on the road to grace and salvation.

- Kvetching will not cure your addictions. In fact, many who promote self-help, especially those who promote some form of "recovery," will probably say that kvetching is itself an addiction that requires a 12-step recovery program.

In short, kvetching will not make your life any less hard. Kvetching creatively can only make your burdens a little more bearable. Given how hard life is, that's not a bad bargain.

THE VIRTUES OF KVETCHING

The virtues of kvetching are modest, but that's no reason to dismiss them.

- Kvetching creatively can give you a way to unburden yourself to others without driving them away. This is no small accomplishment.

- Kvetching creatively can give you some unexpected friends—other creative kvetchers and those who aspire to be creative kvetchers! I have found that some—but certainly not all—people are intrigued by my philosophy of life and the kvetching that follows from it. Some have actually asked for kvetching lessons.

- Kvetching creatively can help you stop pretending everything is okay when (of course) it isn't. This in itself should give you some relief from the burdens of life.

- Kvetching creatively can help you see your problems more realistically. First, kvetching can help you express your problems instead of denying them. Second, if you're lucky enough to kvetch to a perceptive and honest listener, you may even get some useful feedback. This is an added bonus.

39

- Unlike therapy and many other things in life, kvetching creatively is absolutely free!

A WORD ABOUT REALITY, HOPE, AND ACTION

Life is hard. But that's not our real problem. Our real problem is the pressure to pretend that life is not hard. A solution to the real problem is to resist the pressure, to fight back, to say we just won't take it anymore. In other words, a solution to the real problem is to realize that we're all entitled to kvetch, and then to go ahead and do it as creatively as possible.

The people who have objected most strongly to my philosophy of life usually do so for a variety of reasons. But their objections often fall into these four categories:

Objection 1. *If we don't have a positive attitude, we won't be happy or achieve our goals in life.*

Here's my response:

It's the relentless push for a positive attitude in the face of adversity that is overwhelming and overburdening us. When we're faced with a difficulty, large or small, a positive attitude may be nothing more than denial of a real problem. At the very least, it can prevent us from seeing what's right in front of our eyes.

Remember my friend Fred, the one whose boss was giving him a hard time? Fred had such a positive attitude (before he learned to kvetch) that he could not see—until it was much too late—that his boss wasn't exactly thrilled with him from the start. He turned down good job offers because he couldn't see that things weren't going to get better. Even the poorest kvetcher could have seen what was coming from a mile away. After Fred got another job (a much better one, I'm happy to say), he regretted that he had pretended to himself that his boss really appreciated him. Fred is now a regular creative kvetcher, but he says he wished he knew about kvetching sooner. Then at least he could have seen the problem from the start. Then he could have made some different decisions along the way.

The freedom to kvetch, then, is not merely a coping mechanism. It comes from an ability to look reality in the eye and see it for what it is. Getting reality right is, in my opinion, the best way to cope with life. Whether or not you choose to kvetch, whether or not you chose to do anything more than kvetch, you need to get reality right. As a therapist, I work hard to help my clients overcome all forms of self-deception.

> Objection 2. *Kvetching is passive. It will stop you from taking positive action.*

My response:

Kvetching is passive only in the sense that the kvetcher may intend to do nothing more about his problem than kvetch about it. And remember, kvetching itself is a perfectly legitimate way to cope with life, as long as the kvetching is creative. Also, there's no reason to think that kvetching prevents us from taking additional action. Consider this example.

In my first physical therapy session for my Achilles tendons, I told my physical therapist, Marilyn, that I was totally demoralized. "I'll never get better," I kvetched.

Marilyn responded in the usual way, by telling me I needed a positive attitude to get better. Actually, what she said was, "None of what we do here will help unless you have a positive attitude."

Now Marilyn is an excellent physical therapist: Many of her patients probably respond well to this positive-attitude stuff. So I couldn't hold that against her. I stuck with her—and I'm glad I did—but her words didn't make much sense to me. If she meant that I needed a positive attitude in order to *do* my painful exercises, she was dead wrong: "You know Marilyn," I began, "I can be as negative, nervous, and worried as hell. I can be the world's biggest pessimist, and still heal—as long as I do my routine every day. It's the *exercises* that will make my tendons heal, right?"

"Of course, Barbara," Marilyn agreed readily. Marilyn

is a smart woman. That's why I don't think she was saying that it was the positive attitude itself that would heal my tendons. She is a *physical* therapist, not a mind therapist, after all. Matter over matter, not mind over matter, I always say. But the point is, my kvetching, my negative attitude, didn't stop me from doing what I needed to do to get better. I am kvetching my way through my exercises. And I have begun to get better, negative attitude and all.

Also remember that kvetching can actually help you see the difficulties of life more realistically. Kvetchers aren't in denial. They don't pretend everything is okay when it's not. And this is important: When you kvetch creatively, your listener can sometimes give you a "reality check" on your problem.

When Fred first came to me with his long list of complaints, I asked him to tell me what had happened at work. Right away I could see that his problem with his boss was not in his head: It sounded as though Fred's boss didn't value him from day one, and I told him so. I think he heard me. I know he heard me. Although it was too late for Fred to take the job offers he had turned down, it wasn't too late for him to find and land another job, which he promptly accepted. Good thing, since he learned he would soon be forced to leave his original job.

Getting reality right is the first step to taking productive action—if there's something you can actually change. Of course, too often the situation can't be changed. This is why I hate life. In any case, kvetching doesn't prevent action. It may help you take more effective action, when you want to do more than kvetch. Kvetching may be the first step on the road to more realistic action.

Objection 3. *My philosophy of life is a hopeless one.*

My response:

This argument always amuses me. After all, at the very least kvetchers expect *someone* to care enough about them to listen to their kvetching. There's lots of hope in that expectation alone. And kvetching creatively is a good way to connect with others. There's hope in that too. Moreover, being realistic about life isn't the same as being hopeless. Some things can be changed, others can't. It is, as the saying goes, important to know the difference. But it's just as important to be free to kvetch—in either case.

And remember: Kvetching doesn't stop you from having fun at the same time. In fact, creative kvetching is fun.

Objection 4. *My philosophy of life is unrealistically pessimistic, since life can go well.*

My response:

We don't need to deny what's right or good about life.

Sometimes things do turn out okay, sometimes more than okay—even for me. But can we count on that to last? Does having something go well guarantee that it will continue on that way? Let's be realistic.

I confess. I may have a slightly pessimistic bias. Then again, maybe not. Whatever my bias, don't rely on me. Ask yourself this question: How many people want an honest answer to the question "How are you?" How many people want to hear all about your problems when they ask you how you are? How many people insist that you kvetch? Not many, I bet. That's because in America the demand for a positive attitude is real.

CHAPTER 3

OBSTACLES TO CREATIVE KVETCHING, OR, THE TYRANNY OF THE POSITIVE ATTITUDE

I live in Yankee territory—the coast of Maine. Sometimes it seems as American as living in a Norman Rockwell painting. Well, almost. Not as American as living in Nebraska, which I did for five long years. But much more American than living in the Bronx, which is where I started out, or in Houston, where I spent one very long year. It's been instructive to learn how Americans from all parts of the country react to my philosophy of life. But Mainers are especially interesting to me, since they pride themselves on their understated, no-nonsense approach to life. That brings me to Phil, a fellow in our neighborhood.

Phil is a regular guy—a real American, an accountant

47

with a wife, two kids, three pets, and a mortgage. He has a shed for his snow blower and lawn mower, a wood stove, and a pickup truck. He hunts and fishes, and even goes ice fishing in the winter—Phil is no wimp. He has a great sense of humor and likes to spend time with the guys. Phil also likes to complain. We have great fun complaining to each other. So I was caught off guard when he greeted me one day with the usual, "How are you?," and I told him for the first time, "To be honest, I really hate life."

"You don't mean that, Babs!" Phil said nervously, the ready smile gone from his face.

"I do, really, I do; let me tell you why," I answered, and proceeded to explain my philosophy of life.

"Well, you may *think* that, but you can't *say* that." Phil was now visibly upset; I obviously had struck a nerve.

"Why not, Phil? What about *your* favorite saying?" I was more than a little curious, since Phil often says, "Life's a bitch—and then you die." It's true that he always says this with a smile, with good humor. But he says it nonetheless, especially when things aren't going his way. It's Phil's way of kvetching, I think.

"Well, I'm just *joking* when I say that." Phil sounded defensive.

"But it sounds to me like you mean it when you say it," I countered.

"Yeah, but it's not the same as saying you *hate* life.

Life is wonderful. You can't say you hate something wonderful. You can say you hate something awful, but not something wonderful."

What happened here? Obviously, I had stumbled onto something sacred, but Phil isn't a spiritual kind of guy. So I don't think I offended his religious sensibilities. No, I had committed blasphemy of another sort. It was secular blasphemy, as if I had blasphemed America itself. Here in America we have a good life—the *best* life, according to many, and certainly according to Phil. Saying you hate life is like saying you hate America and apple pie, or so I concluded.

I'm happy to say that, after many long discussions, Phil now "gets" my point of view. He's no longer upset by my pronouncements about life. He prefers to stick with his "Life's a bitch," but what's wrong with that? We each must kvetch in our own way (although Phil denies that he's kvetching when he says that). Still, Phil's reaction to my philosophy of life is not unique. Here's a small sample of what others have said (and they're not just Mainers):

- *"You can't really mean what you say about life, or you'd be depressed, and you're not depressed (or unhappy, miserable or whatever). You have too much fun to hate life."*

49

My response:

"Just because I hate life doesn't mean I can't have fun. I can hate the way 'the system' works, and still have some fun within it."

- *"You can't really hate life or everything, because you like me."*

My response:

"Yes, I do like you. But you're just *you*, you're not life, you're not everything. You're not *the system*." (This one always gets a little too philosophical for most people.)

- *"You can't really hate life because life doesn't always go badly. Things can and do go well."*

My response:

"True, but the problem is there's no guarantee. That's the problem with the system, the problem with life."

Some people try to write me off: They take me to be joking, and they laugh, or they just ignore me when I kvetch about life, or they lecture me about the dangers of negativity, or they keep their distance. But no matter what, they seem just a little nervous. I'm obviously saying something that JUST ISN'T SAID. Certainly not here. And certainly not by someone who's not down and out—at least not yet.

People keep rejecting my philosophy until life hands them a mess that optimism or denial won't fix. Then, sometimes, they come around—like my friend Andrea, who, in a moment of "weakness," blurted out that she hated life too. Of course, I see that as a moment of strength, but we'll let that pass. Unlike Andrea, some have stuck with their kvetching for more than a day. Some have actively sought me out for kvetching lessons. Some of my friends have formed a kvetching club. People are crying out for help. If you want to kvetch about life in American—not "recover" from life, but kvetch about it!—there are no support systems to help you out. Need proof? Answer this question: Where are all those self-help books on kvetching?

No doubt about it. Americans face many obstacles to creative kvetching. In the rest of this chapter, I list the five most serious ones.

OBSTACLE 1: AMERICAN HISTORY

How did Americans get so hooked on a positive attitude? You don't need a history lesson to answer that question. Remember our British ancestors? They brought with them that famous British "stiff upper lip." Still, to be fair, we can't put all the blame on them. After all, the American Revolution did start out with a lot of kvetching: Remember "No Taxation Without Representation"? Now there's a great example of world-class kvetching, and kvetching that didn't prevent taking action, to boot! So our founding fathers and mothers had *some* kvetching ability—at least a little, at least to begin with.

But somewhere along the way, something went wrong. I suggest this: Early on, America billed itself as the land of opportunity. Remember the Western Frontier and the Gold Rush? Remember the stories about the immigrants getting their first glimpse of the Statue of Liberty? Remember all those Horatio Alger rags-to-riches stories? From the beginning, America has been famous as the place where "anything-is-possible-if-you-try-hard-enough." That's the American Dream. The American Dream is anti-kvetching. Even though the Dream gets exposed over and over as nothing but myth, you don't see signs of Americans' giving up on it. American optimism is our biggest claim to fame.

OBSTACLE 2: AMERICAN PSYCHOLOGY

Why do so many Americans insist that we smile and act happy when we're not? What, psychologically speaking, might motivate that anti-kvetching attitude? Two explanations occur to me:

Obstacles to Creative Kvetching

1. Isn't it easier for people not to listen? Lots of people want to pretend everything is okay; hearing you kvetch makes them nervous. It may remind them that things really aren't okay, that they have real problems, too—like my friend Andrea or my neighbor Phil. They prefer the pretense—as long as it works, that is. Then they crack.

2. Then there are those who don't want to listen to you—period. They're not in denial, they're just selfish. After all, most people don't want to hear other people's problems. Most people want to talk about their *own* problems. So most people want to *be* the kvetchers, not the listeners. Yet many of those same people demand a positive attitude, but only in *others*, not in themselves. And why shouldn't they feel this way? It gives them lots of listeners for their own kvetching, kvetching which, by the way, they often deny. (More about Kvetchers in Denial in Chapter 6.) Yet those same people, the ones who kvetch loudest but deny that they are kvetching, are sometimes the ones who push the hardest for a positive attitude—in everyone else, of course.

When you think about it, it's no wonder that we all need so many therapists. We have to pay people to listen to us kvetch, because there are so many kvetchers and so few listeners. We have to pay people to be our Professional Kvetching Listeners. We can go to therapy and kvetch with perfect confidentiality, and then pretend to everyone else that we're not kvetching at all. We can pretend that we have a positive attitude when we have no such thing.

Are most Americans closet kvetchers? If so, there's hope for us yet.

OBSTACLE 3: AMERICAN PSYCHOTHERAPY

I hate to list professional psychotherapy among my obstacles to creative kvetching. After all, I am a professional psychotherapist. I believe in the value of professional therapy, both as a practitioner and as a consumer: There are times, lots of times, when self-help books just won't do the job, even self-help books about kvetching. Still, I see problems.

Here's an obvious problem: Therapists may listen patiently (and confidentially) to their clients' kvetching. They may even encourage their clients to kvetch to them freely and openly. That's what therapy is for, right? But sooner or later even the most patient therapist gets tired of all the kvetching. This we call professional burnout. I think the burnout has to do with the fact that therapists are on the receiving end of all that kvetching. Let's face it, kvetching back at your clients is just not considered acceptable therapeutic behavior, at least not in most professional circles. I myself have done it only on rare occasions, and then only with lots of forethought. No, there's no balance of kvetching give and take in the consultation room. He who pays the piper gets to kvetch. So even if all Americans had their own therapist to kvetch to, sooner or later they would wear those therapists out. Then whom could they kvetch to—without blowing their smiley-face image?

And even if therapists could tolerate an endless amount of kvetching, even if they encouraged their clients to kvetch to them more often, even if they didn't burn out, even if they kvetched back, a less obvious problem lurks in the background. It is this: I don't know a single type of therapy that teaches clients how to kvetch creatively in *real life*. And real life is, after all, where kvetching really counts. It's one thing to kvetch to your therapist, where you don't have to be particularly creative about it, because you're *paying* to kvetch. Your therapist *has* to listen. It's quite another to kvetch to your friends, coworkers, and family. There you can get into real trouble, especially if you don't know how to kvetch creatively, especially if they can't tolerate anything but a positive attitude. They don't have to listen. They can stop you right in your kvetchy tracks. You could end up needing a therapist.

AMERICAN PSYCHOTHERAPY

"I feel we've had a good session today."

OBSTACLE 4: AMERICAN SELF-HELP

By now you may be thinking, "Wait a minute! *What* are you talking about? America has no anti-kvetching attitude? What about all those support groups, where people get together and *kvetch* about everything, from their love and shopping addictions to their co-dependency? What about those daytime-TV talk shows, where all those people love to air their dysfunctional families before millions of hungry viewers? What about all that public complaining going on in the name of 'recovery'? What about the bigger and bigger section of bookstores devoted to 'self-help'?"

I confess, you've got a point. Being a victim is fashionable in America these days. So fashionable, in fact, that we're all in danger of being "in denial" if we don't proclaim ourselves the member of some victim category and then join a 12-step recovery program or some kind of support group, or at least buy a self-help book. No, this certainly sounds like there's a whole lot of kvetching going on.

But is there? Look closer. Behind all that alleged kvetching is the most positive, optimistic attitude imaginable. In her book *I'm Dysfunctional, You're Dysfunctional*, Wendy Kaminer documents this trend as she dissects the recovery movement and other self-help trends, from Norman Vincent Peale's 1952 book, *The Power of Positive Thinking*, to Werner Erhard's est, the codependency movement, Adult Children of Alcoholics, and so on. Just follow the twelve steps, think positive thoughts, listen to your inner child (or whatever the expert's "self-help" advice is), and you too can be whole, happy, self-directed, rich, loved . . . You fill in the blank. You don't have to think for yourself, Kaminer explains. It's all laid out for you, in advance, with lots of guarantees. Show and tell, and then everything is A-okay. Go on TV, and confess to having a dark past (or present), and then you get "closure." In my opinion, this isn't kvetching—it's *pseudokvetching*.

Don't get me wrong. Like Wendy Kaminer, I'm happy for those who have gotten real help, better lives, from any of these movements. But if you want to learn to kvetch— really kvetch—they won't help you. You won't learn the real thing in those groups.

That's because real kvetching has a very different philosophy behind it. Remember, we're *all* victims of life, because life is hard for everyone. We don't have crystal balls to tell us what life has in store for us (which is probably a good thing). Real kvetchers know that there's no BIG ANSWER to life's many problems, because life is inherently problematic. Life is *never* okay. Sometimes, it's just a little less not-okay. Creative kvetching can make life a little less not-okay. That's why I make such limited claims for kvetching—even for creative kvetching.

Not convinced? Consider the titles of recent self-help books. Here's a small sample: *Spontaneous Optimism, The Pursuit of Happiness, Prescriptions for Happiness, You Can*

Be Happy No Matter What, Happiness Is a Choice, When Am I Going to Be Happy?, Shortcuts to Bliss, Happiness in 30 Days or Less, 30 Days to Happiness. Nowhere is America's positive attitude expressed more clearly than inside the covers of self-help books. If you find joy between the covers (of those books, that is) good for you, but that has never worked for me. I need to kvetch. Maybe it's genetic.

OBSTACLE 5: AMERICAN BIOLOGY

On November 29, 1996, *The New York Times* reported the discovery of a new gene that determines our behavior. You probably know that many forms of behavior—from drinking and criminality to sex and eating (to name a few)—have all, at one time or another, been blamed on some gene. But in 1996, the discovery of a gene for worry, anxiety, and pessimism was reported. Even the *Times* itself used the word "kvetch" to describe the people who might have this gene. Therefore, I'm probably not stretching science too far when I say that the gene for kvetching may have been discovered—I'll call it the "kvetching gene."

Here's my thought. Maybe Americans tout optimism for reasons that transcend their history, psychology, psychotherapy, and self-help. Maybe Americans are KVETCHING-CHALLENGED by biology, through no fault of their own. Most Americans, that is.

Stop Smiling, Start Kvetching

AMERICAN SELF-HELP

POSITIVE THOUGHT
AFFIRMATION THERAPY
SELF-HELPING
MORE JOY
EVERY DAY, EVERY WHICH WAY
CENTERING
MEDITATIONS
A NEW BEGINNING
FREE TO BE

MANKOFF

Obstacles to Creative Kvetching

Of course I'm not kvetching-challenged. Nor are the many New Yorkers I grew up with or have come to know. How did *they* get the "kvetching gene"? Well, a good chunk of New Yorkers are Jewish, and this may give them an edge. Still, we don't know if the edge is biological, psychological, or sociological. After all, Jewish mothers can transmit a talent for kvetching even if their children are adopted—although, to be honest, I don't know any studies that compare the kvetching of the biological children of Jewish mothers to a control group of adopted children of Jewish mothers. And lots of non-Jewish New Yorkers are great kvetchers.

Let me think about the places outside of New York where I have lived. Mainers aren't good kvetchers—remember Phil? Nor are Nebraskans. And Texans, well, can you even picture a Texan kvetching? New Jerseyites can kvetch pretty well; but most of them are transplanted (or wannabe) New Yorkers. So they don't count.

But the fact that New Yorkers are the best kvetchers I know doesn't make their kvetching a biological fact. For starters, we don't yet have the "Kvetching Gene Home Diagnostic Test Kit." And I don't know how well the gene for worry, pessimism, and anxiety has held up in further scientific tests. If you want scientific controversy, claim a gene controls behavior. You'll never get much consensus on that. And to complicate matters more, many (I mean *many*) New Yorkers do not (I repeat, *do not*) know how to kvetch *cre-*

AMERICAN BIOLOGY: THE KVETCHING GENE

atively. So even if they do have the "kvetching gene," that's no guarantee that they are *creative* kvetchers.

My point is this: Even if kvetching has a genetic component, that doesn't mean it can't be learned. Remember, I have taught Mainers, Nebraskans, and even Texans how to kvetch. And they're all pretty kvetching-challenged. Nope—anatomy is not destiny, at least not when it comes to kvetching. That's the most optimism I've ever been able to conjure up, because I really believe that *anyone* who wants to learn to kvetch can do it. And help is on the way. Just turn the page to start the 5-Step Guide to Creative Kvetching.

PART II

THE 5-STEP GUIDE TO CREATIVE KVETCHING

CHAPTER 4

STEP 1: YOUR INALIENABLE RIGHT TO KVETCH

When I first injured my Achilles tendons, I got pretty depressed about the whole thing. Actually, it was a re-injury: I had torn them this way ten years ago, so I knew how long and painful the physical therapy would be. I knew how long it would be before I could move around normally. I knew how poorly I would cope. Physical endurance is just not one of my strengths. Naturally, I started kvetching.

First I kvetched to my husband David.

"It's lousy for sure," he said. I knew he meant it would be lousy for both of us. After all, he had had to live with me through the last round of injury and physical therapy. He knew how much of a pain I could be. "But look on the bright side," he continued, "you got better last time, and this time you know how to do the physical therapy right."

Was I hearing correctly? My own husband telling me to

"cheer up and look on the bright side"? Twenty-four years of listening to me kvetch, twenty-four years of hearing my philosophy of life, and he's telling me IT'S NO BIG DEAL? And after I taught *him* how to kvetch?

"David, what are you telling me?" I was asking him to rethink his position, *seriously* asking.

A look of terror followed by understanding crossed his face. "I'm sorry, Barbara, really, really, sorry. My mistake here. You're right. It's going to be long and miserable. You can kvetch to me about it, but I can only give you about fifteen minutes. Then I have to get some work done."

That was a close call. Not only had I retorn my Achilles tendons, but for a minute there I thought my marriage was in jeopardy. But no, my marriage could be saved. David might be kvetching-challenged by birth—he is a WASP, after all—but he had learned to overcome that problem over the years (in fact, he was my first kvetching student). David was just having a *momentary* relapse. We could recover from this.

"Actually, I think five minutes of concentrated kvetching will do for now." I didn't want to be a hog. I didn't want to risk being a noncreative kvetcher at such a delicate moment. And just knowing that David understood that I needed to kvetch helped me feel better. After kvetching for just two minutes, even my Achilles tendons started to hurt a little less.

Then I kvetched to my doctor, Bryce, the one who wants

to be reincarnated as a rock, because he doesn't like to take chances.

"Enthesopathy," Bryce pronounced. "That's what you have. It's lots of little tears where the tendon inserts into the heel bone. Let me explain." And Bryce proceeded to tell me what a lousy injury this was. How his other enthesopathy patients took between six and twelve months (or more) to heal. How demoralizing it was. How I'd probably want to give up on the physical therapy, because I would see no progress for weeks at a time. You'd think that this would have made me more depressed, but quite the opposite occurred.

"I know all this from last time, Bryce, but just hearing you say it again helps a lot."

"I know, Barbara. It took you years to get me trained, to whip me into shape, but I finally get it. There's no use in telling you it's no big deal when we both know better. Besides, you'll kill me if I say that." Bryce may not have learned to kvetch himself, but he gets lots of credit for having learned not to deny my right to be miserable.

"Of course, Barbara, sooner or later, you will recover from this, again." Bryce was taking a big risk here, and he knew it. The faint smile gave him away.

"Oh, I know that," I conceded, "and I can even cope with that knowledge. So long as I can kvetch every step of the way."

"Deal."

NO LIFE PROBLEM IS TOO TRIVIAL TO KVETCH ABOUT

If you want to learn to kvetch, the biggest hurdle to overcome is your belief that you have to be terminally ill before you can kvetch. You have to overcome your deeply felt sense that unless you're dying, *your* problems in life just don't measure up. After all, if you are reading this book, you probably aren't starving to death, or a political prisoner, or worse. And even if you were, lots of people would question your right to kvetch. So you're probably thinking, "What right do I have to be upset about a bad day at the office, or about the dishwasher breaking down again, or the argument with my best friend?" How can you compare yourself with people who have *real* trouble? Remember my friend Fred?

My mother is my role model. She knows how to kvetch. And she doesn't let *anyone* tell her that her problem is too trivial to merit kvetching. Not anyone. For instance, the other day she went to the oral surgeon for some gum surgery. Needless to say, she was pretty upset about the whole ordeal, and she expressed her fears to the dentist. Actually, she kvetched to him. A lot. Did he listen sympathetically? Absolutely not. He said, "What are you so upset about? It's *only* your gums. It's not like you're in for heart surgery." This didn't daunt my mother. She replied, "Yeah, well, it may not be heart surgery, but it's *my* gum surgery, and I'm upset about it." This is not a woman who is kvetching-challenged. Then

70

again, she is not the typical American: She's a native New York.

If you are an American, reclaiming your inalienable right to kvetch may be the hardest thing you will ever try to do. Realizing that no problem is too trivial to kvetch about might be the hardest thing you will ever try to do even if you are an American from New York City—even if you are a Jewish American from New York City and think you're not kvetching-challenged at all.

Why is this so hard? You already know the answer: American History, American Psychology, American Psychotherapy, American Self-Help, and American Biology. They all conspire against kvetching. So if you want to kvetch, you have to be determined. And if you want to kvetch creatively, you have to be skilled. In this chapter, we work on your kvetching determination. In the chapters that follow, we work on your kvetching skills.

HIGH-CLASS WORRIES

David and I first met about the time I was applying to graduate schools in psychology. At first I kvetched that I wouldn't get into a good program. Then, having gotten into several, I kvetched about not knowing which one to accept. I still remember the moment David looked up at me and dismissed my worry (and my kvetching) with six words: *"This is a high-class worry."*

"What's a high-class worry?" I asked. "Is this one of your sociology concepts?"

"Probably, since it came from a friend who grew up poor and went on to become a sociologist. But I find it useful. In this theory, worries can be arranged along a continuum, from the most low-class, or serious, worry, up to the most high-class, or trivial, worry. The most low-class worry might be something like this: You have been taken hostage by terrorists who will shoot you in one minute if their impossible demands aren't met. The most high-class worry might be trying to figure out how to spend the millions you just won in the lottery. Imagine all the deserving charities, long-lost relatives, and IRS agents you would have to deal with. Of course, a worry can fit anywhere along the continuum between those two extremes, depending on how serious, how high-class or low-class, it is. The important point is that no matter how serious the worry is or isn't, it's still *your* worry. It's still a worry, and you have every right to have it and to worry it to death and kvetch about it. But identifying a problem as relatively high-class or low-class can be helpful to keep it in perspective. Then you won't worry too much about the less serious worries."

He sat back and beamed, as if he had contributed some real pearl of wisdom. I could see he was really trying, but he had missed something important.

"Not bad for a kvetching-challenged guy," I said. "At least you've got it half right."

"Only half right?" David looked surprised.

"You're right that every problem, no matter how important or how trivial, is still a problem, so you have the right to worry about it and kvetch about it. But this business of 'don't sweat the small stuff'—that's dead wrong. That's the problem I'm trying to combat. That sounds like an American commandment, 'Thou shalt not kvetch about the more trivial problems.' And who gets to decide what are high-class and what are low-class worries, anyway? It sounds like anyone can remove your right to kvetch by deciding your problem is a high-class worry, and then dismissing it." I was on a roll, but I paused for breath.

"Let me put it this way," I continued. "A high-class worry is a worry that *someone else* has but that *you* don't have. And it's *you*, not the person with the problem, who gets to decide that it's no big deal. Am I close?"

David's smile faded quickly. He knew when he was beaten.

I concede this point: There really are more serious and less serious worries in life. By all objective standards, gangrene is worse than a hangnail; not getting into any graduate school is worse than not knowing which graduate school offer to accept; not having enough food is worse than not knowing which restaurant to go out to—and so on and so on.

But you get my point. You can always point to someone whose problems are worse than yours, in many cases, probably much worse. You can also always point to someone who's better off in whatever way you feel unfortunate. Sure, I got into four good graduate programs. But my friend Larry got into five. See? Even though there's an objective pecking order in the world of troubles, the idea of high-class and low-class worries has some relativity built into it. After all, it depends on whom you're comparing yourself with.

And of course, all those well-meaning friends are likely to rig the game, by comparing you to someone with lower-class worries so that your problems look trivial in comparison. Anti-kvetching Americans use this technique to keep others from kvetching. They appeal to the virtues of a positive attitude. But really, underneath all that nonsense, they are telling you that you don't deserve to kvetch, because your problems are just not that serious. Naturally, these are the very same people who think that *their* problems are always serious.

When you can recognize this maneuver for what it is, you have taken the first step to reclaiming your inalienable right to kvetch.

HOW TO RECLAIM YOUR INALIENABLE RIGHT TO KVETCH

The Inalienable Right to Kvetch may not appear explicitly in the Constitution (or even in the Declaration of Independence), but it's as important as anything in the Bill of Rights. And while I'm no lawyer, it seems to me that kvetching is protected by the First Amendment—Freedom of Speech surely includes Freedom to Kvetch. After all, wasn't our country founded by first-rate kvetchers? Recall your American history. Our founding fathers (and mothers) kvetched about "Taxation Without Representation." Then they wrote the Declaration of Independence—they actually kvetched *in writing*. And they went to *war*. See, kvetching doesn't stop you from taking action. Remember, the American Revolution began with kvetching.

So we didn't start out kvetching-challenged at all. But somewhere along the way, we became kvetching-challenged. Maybe we got complacent—once we got rid of the British. Maybe American Biology won out in the end. Whatever went wrong, it's time to make a fresh start.

The following steps will help you reclaim your inalienable right to kvetch. Once you feel free to kvetch, you can go on to learn how to kvetch.

1. Diagnose Your Anti-Kvetching Attitude

The very first step to take is this: Figure out whether you have an anti-kvetching attitude. This is not as easy as it may seem, because many Americans *think* they can accept kvetching when they cannot—not even in themselves. Many Americans are not consciously aware of just how much they have learned, accepted, tolerated, or inherited a positive attitude toward life.

To determine whether you have an anti-kvetching attitude, answer the following questions:

- Do you try to look on the bright side?
- Do you tell yourself, "It's no big deal"?
- Do you feel guilty or bad for feeling bad?
- Do you agree with people who tell you to cheer up because "it's not that bad"?
- Do you try to convince others to cheer up because "it's not that bad"?

If you answered "yes" to *any* of the above questions, you probably have an anti-kvetching attitude, and you need to go to the next step and declare your independence. If you answered "no" to all of the above questions, you have no motivational obstacle to learning how to kvetch creatively, and so you can proceed directly to Chapter 5.

2. Make Your Declaration of Independence

There's no better way to reclaim your inalienable right to kvetch than to do it—just do it. It's not easy. It's very, very hard. But it can be done. To get started, you might consider making yourself a "certificate" to hang on the wall.

Something like this: Sally Smith Hereby Declares Her Inalienable Right to Kvetch. If you're feeling brave, put the certificate in some obvious spot, a place where others can see it and ask you about it. If you're not that brave, it's okay to put it out of view—as long as *you* can see it, of course.

For now, here are the things you need to tell *yourself*. We'll discuss how you should actually deal with *other* people in Chapters 5 to 8.

Just say "NO"—Just say "NO MORE"!

- No more trying to look on the bright side no matter what.
- No more telling yourself that "it's no big deal" when it *is* a big deal.
- No more feeling guilty or bad for feeling bad.
- No more agreeing with people who tell you that "it's not that bad."
- No more convincing others that "it's not that bad."

Just say "YES"!

- Yes, I have the right to see my problem as a real problem.
- Yes, I have the right to say "it's a big deal" when it is to me.

- Yes, I have the right to feel bad when I feel bad.
- Yes, I have the right to disagree with people who tell me that "it's not that bad."
- Yes, I should stop convincing others that "it's not that bad."

REMEMBER:

- Your worry is *your* worry. Even if others see it as trivial or high-class, it's your worry and you have a right to it.
- You are allowed to feel bad about whatever you feel bad about.

DON'T FORGET:

- You can kvetch and still take additional action about your problem.
- The freedom to kvetch can help you see your problem more realistically.
- You can kvetch and still have fun while you're kvetching.

AND IF ALL ELSE FAILS:

- Life is hard—for everyone.

CHAPTER 5

STEP 2: YOU CAN'T KVETCH TO ALL OF THE PEOPLE ALL OF THE TIME

This morning I went for a walk. Okay, so my Achilles tendons are a *little* better. But before you say "gotcha," you should know that frequent walks are now part of my physical therapy routine.

When I got back to my own neighborhood, I spotted Phil working in his yard (an activity he hates—he jokes about this by calling himself Harry Homeowner). You remember Phil. He's the guy who likes to say "Life's a bitch," but who got upset whenever I said, "I hate life." Phil can tolerate that now, although I'm still not sure he's thrilled with it.

"Hi, Phil. Looks like Harry Homeowner's out and about." I knew that wouldn't upset him.

"Yeah, unfortunately for me, Babs." Phil was kvetching. This was a good sign. "So how are you?" he added.

My God, I thought. He's giving me an opening to kvetch. Should I go for it? Why not? Let's see what happens. "Well, since you asked . . ."

"Yes?" Phil was ready and willing to listen.

"I can't figure out how to start Chapter Five of my new book on 'Kvetching.' Got any suggestions?" Two months earlier I had told Phil about this book, but he showed little interest in it. Recall that serious kvetching was just not his thing. So asking him to actually *help* with a book that encouraged people to kvetch was asking for a lot.

"What's Chapter Five about?" he asked with interest.

"It's about how you can't kvetch to all of the people all of the time. You know how some people are put off if you try to kvetch to them. Some people just don't want to hear it. In my book, I'm trying to teach people to kvetch in ways that don't get them rejected." I was trying not to make this personal, given our earlier struggles.

Phil smiled. I felt encouraged. Why not ask for Phil's help? After all, he knew what it felt like to be put off by someone's (by *my*!) kvetching. And technically, I wasn't merely kvetching to him now. I was actually asking for his help. "Got any suggestions?" I asked as nonchalantly as I could.

"Well," Phil paused, "you've got to have some sort of a test. Something that lets you know whether someone can stand to listen to you kvetch right off the bat."

"Exactly," I replied. I was impressed with Phil's keen

insight. "But what?"

"How about this. You know how we always greet each other with the standard, 'Hi, how are ya?'" I nodded. "Well, when someone says that to you, you can say, 'Not so great,' and see how they take it. Do they ignore you? Do they pretend you said 'fine'? Do they ask to hear more? That's the test."

"Perfect!" I exclaimed. And to myself I thought, Wow! He gets it! He really gets it! Aloud I added, "You're a lifesaver, Phil. I can't thank you enough. But now I better move along and get this into the computer."

"Anytime, Babs."

"And by the way, you're the star of Chapter Three, you know." Was I pushing it?

"Okay, but if your book takes off, I want royalties." That's Phil, ever the accountant.

"Fair enough," I replied.

What happened here? How did we go from Phil's being upset by my kvetching, to his listening to me kvetch and then *helping* me with my book on kvetching? It was true that I hadn't used the offending "I hate life." But still, this was progress.

Only one answer makes sense to me. In the last two years I had stopped telling Phil, "I hate life." I didn't pretend to be okay around him, but I didn't use my usual repertoire of kvetching devices either. As I explained earlier, we had reached a certain unstated agreement. I had respected his right not to tolerate my kvetching, at least certain forms of it. I had respected Phil's anti-kvetching attitude. And now here he was, not only listening to me kvetch about my kvetching book, but helping me teach others how to kvetch creatively. There's a lesson in this, I thought. Let's see if I can pass it on to you.

WHAT ABOUT YOUR INALIENABLE RIGHT?

By now you're probably thinking, "Wait a minute. What happened to my inalienable right to kvetch? I took Step 1 seriously. I believe I have the right to kvetch, even when my worry seems like it's high-class. And now she's telling me I can't kvetch to all of the people all of the time? What's going on here?"

And you know, you're right to kvetch about this. Step 2 does seem to contradict Step 1. But—and stay with me on this—there really is no contradiction. There is no contradiction, because knowing deep down inside that you have the *right* to kvetch and knowing *when* to exercise that right are two entirely different matters. You can, of course, exercise your inalienable right to kvetch whenever you want. It's in the Bill of Rights (or should be)—Freedom of Speech, remember? Kvetching to anyone anytime is *legal*. But you can't kvetch to all of the people all of the time and still kvetch

creatively. You can't be a creative kvetcher if you exercise your inalienable right to kvetch without careful consideration. Legality and creativity are not the same thing. Think about it. You have the *right* to tell your boss he's an idiot, but do you automatically do it? Of course not, unless you want to get fired. You have the *right* to go out in a blizzard without your winter coat, but do you do it? Probably not. Who wants to freeze to death? In short, you don't want the *consequences* of exercising those rights foolishly.

It's the same with kvetching. If you kvetch to the wrong person or to the right person at the wrong time, you might drive that person away. Then you aren't kvetching creatively. So now we confront one of the harshest realities of life: Not everyone can enjoy, or even tolerate, your kvetching. Worse yet, this is true even if your kvetching is done creatively. Therefore it is important for you to learn who can tolerate your kvetching and, even better, to learn who can appreciate your kvetching. This means getting informed consent before you start kvetching. Getting informed consent is just what we work on in this chapter.

Step 2 is a very hard step to take. It may be the hardest step of all. In fact, I'm not sure you can begin to cope with Step 2 until you're got Step 1 nailed down. You need a very firm sense of kvetching entitlement, of your inalienable right to kvetch, before you can learn when *not* to kvetch. So if you're at all shaky on Step 1, go back and work on it—right this minute. If you're firm about your inalienable right to kvetch, proceed to Step 2.

How to Get Informed Consent to Kvetch

It's surprising to discover how many hard-core kvetchers don't have a clue about getting informed consent. Some of the most dedicated kvetchers I know try to kvetch to all of the people all of the time, and they end up driving their listeners away, without knowing why. These people are obviously not kvetching-challenged. Many of them are New Yorkers—I know, I'm one of them. But they are *creatively* kvetching-challenged. They may have the gene for kvetching but not the gene for creative kvetching—if there is such a thing.

Creative kvetchers don't kvetch to unwilling listeners. The best creative kvetchers can tell how willing a potential listener is just by instinct. They don't need to run any explicit tests, like the one my neighbor Phil recommended. Somehow they just know. And if the listener isn't receptive to their kvetching, they just stop. They move on to someone else. They don't push it.

Most of us aren't that instinctively creative. Most of us need guidance in the fine art of assessing someone's willingness to listen to us kvetch. The following steps will give you that guidance.

1. Learn About the Baseline Kvetch Reception Potential (KRP)

A person's kvetch reception potential (or KRP) is simply their ability to tolerate other people's kvetching. Each of us can tolerate other people's kvetching to a greater or lesser extent, and so we each have our own baseline KRP. For example, my friend George can tolerate my kvetching most of the time (actually, he can tolerate just about anyone's kvetching most of the time). So George's baseline KRP is pretty high. My friend Liz, by contrast, can take everyone's kvetching only in the smallest doses. Her baseline KRP is low. Needless to say, people always kvetch to George, and rarely to Liz. So you shouldn't be surprised to learn that George has a few more friends than Liz. I spend lots more time kvetching to George than to Liz. I only kvetch to Liz when I'm desperate.

I don't know whether our baseline KRP is an inherited trait or a product of our environment. Whichever it is, I do know that each person's baseline KRP is fairly stable. We each tend to tolerate or not tolerate other people's kvetching at pretty much the same level throughout our lives. This is true whether or not we ourselves like to kvetch.

Now for the tricky part. Everyone's KRP is pretty much fixed. But everyone's KRP also has some flexibility. It can change for the moment, depending on whose kvetching is being received. For instance, I can listen to my friend Mikey

85

kvetch for long periods of time. But as soon as my friend Arthur starts to kvetch, I run for cover. So my KRP for Mikey is high compared with my KRP for Arthur. What explains my different reactions to the two of them? For starters, Mikey is a creative kvetcher. He doesn't kvetch to me if my KRP seems down. Arthur kvetches to anyone and everyone, regardless of their KRP. This makes Mikey a more creative kvetcher than Arthur. Although I must admit (in defense of Arthur) that Arthur's KRP is extremely high. Arthur can tolerate anyone's kvetching for long periods of time. I admire Arthur's high baseline KRP. It's much higher than mine.

To get a feel for other people's baseline KRPs—or for your own—you need to know the signs of a low KRP. You need to know the "I've-Had-Enough-of-Your-Kvetching" signs. You already know these. They are pretty standard. They are used whenever someone doesn't want to listen to you kvetch anymore. You probably use them yourself when you don't want to listen to someone else kvetch.

Here are the "I've-Had-Enough-of-Your-Kvetching" signs:

- Rolling the eyes

- Changing the subject

- Saying the words "You think you've got problems . . ."

- Saying the words "Stop complaining!"

- Saying the words "Cheer up!"
- Making an excuse to get out of the conversation
- Looking away
- Walking away
- Running Away

If someone does one or more of these after less than one minute of your kvetching, they probably have a low KRP. I say "probably" because they may just be having a bad day. Then again, they may just have a low KRP *for you.* In any case, you need to learn to kvetch more creatively. If someone displays these signs right away, no matter who is kvetching to them, no matter when they're being kvetched to, it's more certain they have a low baseline KRP.

Be honest with yourself. Do you display any of the signs listed above after less than a minute of other people's kvetching? If so, you probably have a low baseline KRP. Then again, you may just be having a bad day. Or you may have a low KRP for some particular person. If so, you need to work on that too.

2. Assess Each Potential Listener's Momentary KRP

Knowing someone's baseline KRP is a good place to

start when you're deciding whether to kvetch to that particular person. That's because it's usually best not to waste your time kvetching to someone with a chronically low KRP.

Still, to be a creative kvetcher, it's not enough to know the baseline KRP of your potential listener. You need to know whether that listener has a high KRP for *you*. And you need to know whether that listener can tolerate your kvetching at the *exact moment* you want to kvetch to him or her. The KRP your potential listener has at the moment you choose to kvetch is their momentary KRP. This is the KRP your listener has at the crucial moment—the moment of truth, the moment when you want that person to listen to you kvetch, to listen *attentively*.

To be a creative kvetcher, you need to check your potential listener's momentary KRP—her KRP just before you kvetch to her. You need to check her KRP *each time* you want to kvetch, so you don't kvetch to an unwilling listener. Remember, kvetching to an unwilling listener is noncreative kvetching—by definition.

To check your potential listener's momentary KRP, do the following:

• Ask your potential listener how her day is going.

If she says it's been a bad day, move on to someone else. If she says it's been an okay day, proceed to the next item. But beware! Many Americans say they're okay when they're not. That's because many Americans are kvetching-challenged.

- Tell your potential listener that you intend to kvetch.

If your potential listener doesn't know about kvetching, explain what it is—very briefly. Say that you would like to complain about your life. Say that you will do this with no plans to solve your problems. Say that you expect no help from the potential listener. All you ask is that he listen, if he thinks he can. Not that just listening is easy. To the contrary, it's hard, very hard. Just listening is much harder than listening and then giving advice. But just listening can often be more helpful.

All this tells your listener that you will give him lots of credit for trying to listen—just listen. Because it is hard. Creative kvetchers always give credit to people who just listen. Noncreative kvetchers never do.

- Ask your potential listener if she thinks she can stand to listen to you kvetch.

Many people will say yes to this, even if they really can't stand to listen to you kvetch. They say yes because your question catches them off guard: They aren't used to being asked this kind of question. And they say yes because they themselves are kvetching-challenged: They don't want to risk looking bad by saying no. They don't want to appear to be kvetching. So you need to be very clear about this: It's okay for your potential listener to tell you that she doesn't think she can stand to listen to you kvetch. You must reassure her that you will not be hurt or offended if her momentary KRP is low. After all, we all have our bad moments. We all have our limits in life.

- Tell your potential listener that you won't kvetch without his informed consent.

- Reassure your potential listener that it's okay if he thinks he can't stand to listen to you kvetch—if he can't give you his informed consent. Tell him that we all have good and bad days. Tell him that we all have our limits in life.

Because people won't believe this, you may need to repeat this step several times. And you need to be convincing. The best way to do that is to have potential listeners who are "backups"—listeners in reserve.

- Keep in mind at least two other potential listeners, whenever you assess someone's momentary KRP.

Doing this will help you accept a no from any one potential listener. If you approach your backups and they say no at that moment, you may have to wait for another day to kvetch. This is hard. Very, very hard. But it's better than becoming a noncreative kvetcher. It's better than driving away the listeners you do have.

A WELL-KEPT "SECRET"

It is very hard to take no for an answer. That's no secret. Here's the secret: When people realize you can take no for an answer—really and truly take no—they are more willing to listen to you kvetch. They become more tolerant of your kvetching. Sometimes they become even more appreciative of your kvetching. So getting informed consent to kvetch—*real* informed consent, not just lip service—can increase someone's momentary KRP. It can actually *activate* the KRP of someone who has a baseline KRP of zero.

The reason for this is not hard to figure out. When people know they don't *have* to do something, they feel more okay about doing it. The pressure is off. Think about it. Don't you feel more like doing someone a favor if you don't feel obligated? Feeling obligated creates resistance. This is plain old common sense. But most people forget to use it.

CHAPTER 6

STEP 3: DO NOT PRETEND YOU AREN'T KVETCHING WHEN YOU ARE

During another appointment with Bryce (the doctor), the topic of managed care came up. Actually, I brought it up. I had just recently listened to a specialist, Dr. Kramer (we're not on a first-name basis), kvetch about how managed care was making his practice miserable. Of course, I encouraged Dr. Kramer's kvetching. But he didn't need much encouragement; maybe he's got the "kvetching gene." As proof of that, he positively beamed when I told him what a fine kvetcher he was. When I told him I was writing a book about kvetching, Dr. Kramer said he would be proud to be included in it.

"You should hear Dr. Kramer kvetch about managed care," I commented to Bryce. "I'm impressed with his kvetching ability."

Bryce showed no interest in Dr. Kramer's kvetching ability. Instead he explained how all kinds of specialists are complaining about managed care. "Those specialists have had it pretty soft until now. Not like us primary care providers. We've been in the trenches all along, on call all the time, for a fraction of the pay. Now, finally *they* have to put up with the same conditions, and they're complaining like crazy. They don't get any sympathy from me." Bryce was as calm and rational as ever. Still, I thought I detected the slightest hint of annoyance in his tone.

"Why Bryce," I said with a grin, "I think you're— *kvetching!*" I meant it as a compliment, of course. Bryce is a WASP. As WASPy as can be. I've told him this often. He has even told me some WASP jokes, so I was sure he'd be amused by my pronouncement about his kvetching. Maybe even pleased. I was wrong—dead wrong.

"I am not kvetching!" Bryce said firmly. "I'm just telling you what's been happening in the medical world."

How can we understand this conversation? Was Bryce merely giving me some interesting information? Or was he, as I perceived, actually kvetching? Let's consider both claims.

We'll start with Bryce's point of view. He was indeed giving me information about the state of affairs in medicine and managed care. Surely it's unfair to treat all descriptions of the world as instances of kvetching. After all, the world is a pretty sorry place. To describe it—not complain about it, but just describe it—you must discuss some truly miserable events.

My point is this: Not all negative descriptions of the world are produced by kvetchers. Think about newscasters. They bring you bad news all the time, and no one accuses them of kvetching. What about teachers? Surely they're not kvetching when they recount the less than sterling moments in human history. And accountants, when they give you the bad news about how much you owe the IRS? That can't be kvetching. So likewise, why couldn't I believe that Bryce was just giving me objective facts about medical practice—and nothing more? His tone was certainly dispassionate enough.

Still, I was and am convinced that Bryce was doing his own WASPy version of kvetching. He wasn't *merely* talking about some distant state of affairs, like some ancient history in which he had no personal interest. Bryce seemed *bothered*—at least a little—by all those specialists who had had such a cushy existence for so long. And why shouldn't he be? They had had it easy, and now they had the nerve to kvetch about losing their privileged status. They had the nerve to kvetch about finally having to practice medicine the way *he* had always practiced medicine—and without so much as an ounce of kvetching on his part. Why shouldn't Bryce be annoyed by that? I certainly would be!

So despite his protest, I think Bryce's story really was

a complaint, a personal complaint, a glorious complaint. No doubt about it. If Bryce wasn't fully kvetching, he was at least quasi-kvetching. But I'm sure he'd never agree with me. Remember, Bryce is kvetching-challenged. He took my pronouncement that he was kvetching as a criticism. He could not see it as the compliment—indeed, the high praise—that was intended.

Still, we can't accuse Bryce of *pretending* not to be kvetching when he really was kvetching. If you don't *know* you're kvetching (or even quasi-kvetching), then how can you be guilty of any pretense? So Bryce is not guilty of that offense. But unlike Bryce, you have been reading this book. So you now know what kvetching is. You can't plead ignorance—or innocence—about these matters. If you kvetch but pretend you aren't kvetching, you, unlike Bryce, are guilty as charged.

KIDS: KVETCHERS IN DENIAL

Many kvetchers make the mistake of pretending they don't kvetch. They may, for instance, say they are merely "discussing" their views when in reality they are kvetching. They may even believe their own denial of their kvetching. Why do they engage in this denial? I can think of three reasons:

- They don't understand the concept of kvetching.

Do Not Pretend You Aren't Kvetching

- They don't realize that they are not merely giving information, they are expressing their own personal dissatisfaction with some aspect of life.

- They don't realize that kvetching is a good thing.

We have already considered these reasons in our discussion of Bryce. But now let's take a closer look at the third one. You already know why people fail to see kvetching as good: Most Americans are kvetching-challenged. Remember, American History, Psychology, Psychotherapy, Self-Help, and Biology all conspire to produce the positive attitude that gets in the way of kvetching. They produce America's anti-kvetching attitude. They make it hard for Americans to be proud of their kvetching. So most Americans pretend they aren't kvetching when they really are.

I call people who kvetch but who pretend they are not kvetching KVETCHERS IN DENIAL (or KIDs, for short). They are not to be confused with real children or kids. Real kids are born knowing how to kvetch, even if they don't have the "kvetching gene." Then, when they grow up, many of them learn they shouldn't kvetch. They get socialized into our anti-kvetching society. This happens even to people who may have the "kvetching gene." I say this because some of the biggest kvetchers I know pretend they are not kvetching. They are some of the biggest KIDs on the block.

WHY IT'S BAD TO BE A KID

Denial has its uses. When it works, it's great. I should know, because I don't have much denial. In fact, my husband David says I have none at all. And so I worry and kvetch about *everything*. I mean everything. Like, will lightning strike my house while I'm away and start a fire? It would be nice to be able to deny that aspect of reality now and then. Of course, if I had more denial, I probably wouldn't be such a serious kvetcher—a world-class kvetcher, according to my friend George. George says if they ever have a kvetching competition in the Olympics, I would win, even if I am an American.

But denial has its price. If you have been in therapy or a 12-step program, you have probably heard all about the problems of denial. So I won't review the psychological or self-help literature here. But I will say this: Being a kvetcher in denial is a dangerous occupation—very dangerous.

You already know the reason why. If you kvetch but deny that you are kvetching, you are more likely to annoy your listeners. You are more likely to drive them away. Why? Because you haven't gotten your listener's informed consent. You haven't checked to make sure their KRP is sufficiently high. How can you check your listener's kvetch reception potential if you don't even realize—if you don't even admit—that you are kvetching? Before you check someone's KRP, you have to accept the fact that you kvetch.

Do Not Pretend You Aren't Kvetching

On the other hand, you could luck out. You could deny your kvetching and end up kvetching (in denial) to someone whose baseline KRP is high. Then you probably won't drive that particular listener away. But this kind of luck is rare. In general, you are taking a big risk if you are a kvetcher in denial. There is simply no way to be a KID and still kvetch creatively. Absolutely no way at all. So it's important to admit to yourself and your listener that you are kvetching when that is what you're doing. In the next section I explain how to determine if you are a KID.

HOW TO TELL IF YOU ARE A KID

Here are the five warning signs of being a KID:

- Do people tell you that you complain too much?
- Do people tell you to stop making mountains out of molehills?
- Do people tell you to "cheer up, things will get better"?
- Do people tell you that you never listen to *their* problems?

If you said yes to one or more of these, *and* you maintain that you never (ever) kvetch, you *probably* are a kvetcher in denial. The fifth warning sign is the most definitive one:

- Do you tell people who accuse you of complaining that you aren't complaining, that you're just stating your "views" or just giving an "opinion"?

If you said yes to this question, you are *definitely* a kvetcher in denial. But don't worry, help is on the way.

HOW TO OVERCOME YOUR DENIAL: STOP BEING ASHAMED OF YOUR KVETCHING

Accepting your own kvetching—that is, not being a KID—is easy. But it's easy only if you aren't ashamed of your kvetching. What if you can see that you sometimes kvetch but you can't get past feeling ashamed of it? The following steps should help you conquer your shame about being a kvetcher. Once you can do that, it becomes easier to stop being a KID.

To get over your shame about your kvetching, do the following:

- Understand your shame about being ashamed. Then get over it.

The fact that you are ashamed of your kvetching is nothing to be ashamed of. After all, there are five big obstacles to creative kvetching that work to keep you ashamed. You know them from Chapter 3: American History, American Psychology, American Psychotherapy, American Self-Help, and American Biology. Any one of these can make it hard to let go of your shame about being a kvetcher. But if you have two or more of these obstacles working against you, it's no wonder you're ashamed. Still, you don't have to make the problem worse. Don't be ashamed of your shame.

- Remember that life is hard for everyone.
- Say the following "Affirmations":

    1. Life is hard for everyone, even me (but not especially me).
    2. I have the inalienable right to kvetch.
    3. I want to be a creative kvetcher.
    4. I can be a creative kvetcher.
    5. I deserve to be a creative kvetcher.

HOW TO COPE WITH ANTI-KVETCHERS

What do you do if someone complains about your kvetching? What if someone complains that you are kvetching too much or for no good reason? This is a difficult problem: It's people like this who make you ashamed of your own kvetching. It is people like this who challenge your inalienable right to kvetch. It is people like this who may drive you into denial, into being a KID. I call people who complain about other people's kvetching ANTI-KVETCHERS.

Anti-Kvetchers are tricky to deal with. On the one hand, you don't want to give in to the shame about your kvetching that they can provoke in you. On the other hand, you don't want to kvetch to someone who can't tolerate your kvetching, someone whose KRP toward you is low. If you did that, you wouldn't be kvetching creatively.

And to make matters more confusing, there are two kinds of Anti-Kvetchers: The kind who complain about your kvetching to your face and the kind who complain about your kvetching behind your back. Anti-Kvetchers who complain about your kvetching to your face (I call them Type 1) are not kvetching to you—they are *criticizing* you. Remember, criticizing someone is not the same as kvetching to them. Anti-Kvetchers who complain about your kvetching to *other* people (I call them Type 2) are indeed engaging in bona fide kvetching—about you. Remember, you can only kvetch about one person to another person.

So Anti-Kvetchers are not automatically kvetching-challenged. They themselves may love to kvetch. They are not Anti-Kvetchers when *they* are the ones doing the kvetching. They are Anti-Kvetchers only when it comes to listening to *someone else's* kvetching. They have a kvetching double standard: They may love to kvetch, but they hate to listen to anyone else kvetch. They have a low baseline KRP. Anti-Kvetchers who love to kvetch are probably competitive kvetchers. We talk about competitive kvetching in the next chapter. Right now, let's consider how you can cope with the two types of Anti-Kvetchers.

1. How to Cope with Anti-Kvetchers, Type 2

To cope with Anti-Kvetchers who kvetch about your kvetching behind your back (but not to your face), do the following:

- Decide whether you really want to kvetch to someone who has a low baseline KRP. Is it worth the trouble?

- If you think it's worth a try, tell the person you would like to kvetch to them.

- Do not let on that you know the person is an Anti-Kvetcher—that you know they have been kvetching about you behind your back.

- Ask the person for *permission* to kvetch.

- If permission is given, limit your kvetching to under one minute.

- If permission is not given, accept the refusal. Show you can take no for an answer. Then you should move on. Find someone else to kvetch to.

The goal is simple: You want to raise Anti-Kvetchers' KRP toward you. You also want to give the Anti-Kvetchers less ammunition to use when they kvetch about you behind your back.

2. How to Cope with Anti-Kvetchers, Type 1

Anti-Kvetchers of the first type are easier to spot, since they tell you right to your face that they don't like your kvetching. That makes them more honest than Anti-Kvetchers of the second type. Type 1 Anti-Kvetchers put their cards on the table. I myself prefer to deal with this type. There are no pretenses when you deal with them.

All this means you can be more direct and open with Type 1 than you can with Type 2. To cope with someone who complains about your kvetching directly to you, do the following:

- Realize the person is telling you that their KRP is very low.

- Stop kvetching immediately!

- Acknowledge that yes, you have been kvetching. In other words, don't be a KID.

- Thank the person for telling you that your kvetching is bothering them.

Good manners go a long way here. They disarm your criticizer, because they are unexpected. They stop your criticizer dead in his tracks. They get his attention. No one expects a kvetcher to stop kvetching. No one expects a kvetcher to admit she has been kvetching, and to top it off, to be polite when criticized. No one. This sets a new standard for kvetching etiquette. Go for it.

- Ask the person if they would like to hear the "philosophy of life" that goes along with kvetching.

This is your chance to do a little educating. But first you must get the person's informed consent: Preaching, like kvetching, works best if you have a willing listener.

If the person says no, he doesn't want to hear your philosophy of life, accept his answer and ask him what, if anything, he would like to talk about. In other words, BACK OFF! Don't see this as a sign of defeat. Remember, you must take no for an answer. But take heart: Sooner or later even the worst skeptics come around. You already know why. Even they eventually face situations in life that challenge their anti-kvetching attitude. Remember my friend Andrea? She hated the fact that I said "I hate life"—but only until she hated what was happening in *her* life. Then she said the offending words herself.

If the person says yes, she wants to hear about your philosophy of life, explain the basic premise of this book: That life is hard—for everyone. Even for her. Therefore, we are all entitled to kvetch. Including her. But we should kvetch only to people who want to listen.

- Ask the person if they would like to try kvetching to you.

An invitation to kvetch is rare, and so it may catch the person off guard. But this makes the invitation all the more difficult to resist. Think about it. How often have you been *invited* to kvetch? If your Anti-Kvetcher seems interested but can't think of anything to kvetch about, she probably is a kvetching-challenged Anti-Kvetcher. In that case, offer some suggestions. She can, for instance, kvetch about being kvetching-challenged. Now for the crucial part: If the Anti-Kvetcher does kvetch, you must listen attentively. You must demonstrate what a good KRP looks like. You must be a good role model. You must be the paragon of kvetching etiquette.

ABOUT KILLING TWO BIRDS WITH ONE STONE

You probably can guess what the two birds are. The first bird you've killed by following these instructions is your own shame about your kvetching. (Once you've killed your shame, there's no reason to deny your kvetching. So you can stop being a KID.) The second bird is the low KRP of your anti-kvetching listeners. It's hard for listeners to have low tolerance for someone like you, someone who accepts— someone who respects!—their low kvetching tolerance. This means that the next time you approach these anti-kvetching listeners, there's a good chance their KRP will be a little higher. Maybe even a lot higher. But don't count on it. Not with anyone. Not ever. Not if you want to be a creative kvetcher.

CHAPTER 7

STEP 4: DO NOT BE
A COMPETITIVE KVETCHER

When we were both undergraduates, my friend Lewie used to make jokes about psychotherapy. Since I was a psychology major and Lewie was a journalism major, those jokes were always at my expense, not his. Still, they were funny.

By the time we were seniors, Lewie had developed his own type of "therapy," which he called (not surprisingly) "Lewie Therapy." He also joked about writing a book entitled (not coincidentally) *An Introduction to Lewie Therapy.* Chapter One of Lewie's "book" would be "You Think You've Got Problems!" In that chapter Lewie would describe what to do in the first therapy session with every client.

According to Lewie, in the first session the therapist (also named Lewie) should ask the client what the problem is. No matter what the client answers, the therapist is then instructed to say, "You think *you've* got problems? You shoulda seen what happened to Lewie in Joyzee City last week!"

The theory behind Lewie's question was this: If you help the client realize that Lewie's problems are worse than the client's, the client will feel much better. Lewie thought this was helping his clients put their problems in perspective. Lewie added that you also need to have on hand a spread of great food, since he believed that most emotional problems stem from not being served "nice" food (like the kind your mother cooks for you). That would be Chapter Two of Lewie's book—namely, "Ya Gotta Eat."

"Think it through," Lewie often said. "Whose problems could be worse than Lewie's?"

"So you make your clients feel glad they're not Lewie. Then you give them some nice food. Then they feel better." Lewie had none of the doubts that plagued psychology majors.

"But what if that doesn't do the trick?" I once asked Lewie. I, of course, was worried.

"Aha!" Lewie blurted with confidence. "Then you go to Chapter Three!"

"Which is?"

" 'Come On—Give Lewie a Little Smile.' " Lewie was indeed smiling as he pinched my cheek and anticipated my next question. "You pinch the client on the cheek and say, 'Give Lewie a little smile.' You know, like your great uncle did when you were five and were crying about something. It

Do Not Be a Competitive Kvetcher

"LEWIE THERAPY"

"You think you have problems? My entire wing command was just destroyed."

didn't feel great, but you forgot what you were crying about."

Fortunately for us all, Lewie stuck with journalism. He now has a career in television, not psychotherapy. "Lewie Therapy" may have its merits—humor is not the least of them—but it fails as a guide to creative kvetching. That's because it turns the therapist into a competitive kvetcher. And let's face it, most therapists just don't have Lewie's gift for humor. If they did, they would probably be on TV, on The Comedy Channel. So while "Lewie Therapy" might actually work for *Lewie's* "clients," I doubt that it would work for the rest of us.

WHAT'S A COMPETITIVE KVETCHER?

Many kvetchers are competitive. They repeatedly make the mistake of trying to convince their listeners that their own problems are worse than anyone else's problems. And unlike Lewie, they usually aren't redeemed by their sense of humor. Of course, the problem with claiming that your problems are worse than anyone else's problems is that this claim violates my philosophy of life: That life is hard—*for everyone.*

Remember, we all have an inalienable right to kvetch. We all have the right to kvetch no matter how trivial our problems may seem to others. But we do not have the right to tell other people that *their* problems are trivial, or at least more trivial than our own. Think of it this way: Telling people that their problems are trivial denies them their inalienable right to kvetch. And if you do that, it means you have a low kvetch reception potential. You cannot be a creative kvetcher if you deny the right of others to kvetch—if you have a low KRP. That makes you a competitive kvetcher. Period!

So competitive kvetchers are not creative kvetchers. Competitive kvetchers drive their listeners away. They drive people away by failing to give others credit for having a hard life too. And worse, they hog all the kvetching time. If you hog all the kvetching time, you can't achieve a fair balance of kvetching give and take. Creative kvetchers seek fairness. Competitive kvetchers do not. It's that simple.

WATCH THOSE KPMS

My husband David says that he can tell whether or not I'm feeling okay by checking my KPM rate. KPM stands for Kvetches Per Minute. David says that if my KPM rate is too low, he worries that I may be depressed: I may not have enough energy to kvetch about life. In all fairness, this is unlikely. Since I'm not kvetching-challenged, I need very little energy to kvetch. On the other hand, if my KPM rate is too high, David says he can't stand to listen to me, because I hog all the kvetching time. This gives him no room to kvetch—to counter-kvetch, that is.

Lewie agrees with David about my KPM rate. Neither

David nor Lewie can tell me just what my optimal KPM rate is. But I know I'm kvetching too little when they act worried about me, and too much when they run for cover.

My friend George also monitors my kvetching level, but in a slightly different way. Every day he listens for what he calls my "Kvetch du Jour." If I don't announce one, George gets worried, or so he says. He says that when there is no Kvetch du Jour, he worries that I may be too depressed to kvetch. And if I stick with the same Kvetch du Jour for more than a couple of days, George worries that my problem may be a serious one. So as long as the Kvetch du Jour keeps changing, George says I'm okay.

With David, Lewie, and George listening for the right amount and type of kvetching, who needs therapists? Of course, most Americans are not as fortunate as I am. They don't have people in their lives who take their kvetching seriously—assuming they even know how to kvetch in the first place.

But if you do know how to kvetch, you need to follow one simple rule. You need to watch those KPMs.

HOW TO TELL IF YOUR KPM RATE IS OFF

This is not easy to figure out, especially by yourself. It certainly helps to have friends and family members who can give you the kind of feedback David, Lewie, and George give me. In any case, here are the warning signs to look for.

Do Not Be a Competitive Kvetcher

1. A Low KPM Rate

Your KPM rate may be too low if any of the following applies to you:

- You think life is wonderful, no matter what.

- Your friends marvel at your cheerfulness.

- It never occurs to you to kvetch.

- The thought of kvetching occurs to you, but you dismiss it as bad form.

- You do all the listening and *none* of the kvetching.

2. A High KPM Rate

Your KPM rate may be too high if any of the following applies to you:

- You do all or most of the kvetching and very little listening.

- You feel the urge to kvetch as *soon* as anyone else starts kvetching.

- You think other people's problems are trivial compared with yours.

- You think everyone else kvetches to you too much.

- You resent other people's kvetching.

AVOID THE TEMPTATION

The other day I went to mail a package. Fran, the person who waited on me, is someone I've known for a while. In fact, because Fran is such a friendly, cheerful person, I've put real energy into helping her learn to kvetch—and with some success, I'm happy to say. Fran now kvetches to me regularly. And I kvetch to Fran regularly. We have a nice balance of kvetching give and take. We are not competitive kvetchers. At least not with each other.

But the other day we came close to competitive kvetching. Or at least I did.

"Hi, Fran. How's it going? Got any complaints today?" I never like to leave kvetching to chance.

"Not bad, and you?"

"Same as usual. Got a form for UPS? I need to send out this book today."

"You know the routine, just fill it in," Fran said pleasantly as she handed over the form.

"Fran, I just heard that they changed the department account codes. Is that true?" I was gearing up for some kvetching.

"Yeah," Fran said, with no sign of being disgruntled.

"What a pain. Now I have to learn a new code. I hate that."

"*You* hate that. *You* only have to learn *one* new code. *I* have to learn *five hundred* new codes!"

Let's pause here for reflection. To be honest, I had the urge to get competitive with Fran. I wanted to say something like "Oh, yeah? You think that's bad? You should see how many students enrolled in my classes this term. You should see how much grading I'm going to have to do." You know, something like my version of Lewie's "You think *you've* got problems? You shoulda seen what happened to Lewie in Joyzee City last week!" And I would have felt justified, because Fran was kvetching competitively with me— at least a little, at least I thought so.

But something stopped me. Something nagged at me. What was it? Maybe I didn't want Fran to stop listening to my kvetching. Maybe I didn't want to risk lowering Fran's KRP toward me. And that's exactly what would have happened if I got competitive with her. The competition would escalate, and both of us would end up with lower KRPs for each other. And let's not forget: I *encouraged* Fran to kvetch to me in the first place, so her kvetchy reply to me was a real triumph.

I decided to practice what I preach. Here's what I actually said to Fran:

"Wow! That's really awful. You win. You've got it much

worse than me."

Fran just smiled knowingly. Then I went on to kvetch to her about something else. And Fran was more than happy to listen.

So you see, my motives were not so pure. I wasn't holding back with Fran out of the goodness of my heart. I just realized my own competitive-kvetching instincts. I just avoided the temptation. But this was all in my own interest. After all, I wanted Fran to keep listening to my kvetching. And if truth be told, learning five hundred new codes *is* worse than learning one. Her problem *was* worse than mine. Why not admit it? What did it cost me? Nothing. But I had lots to lose if I got competitive. I could have lost someone whose KRP, at least toward me, is very high. *Creative kvetchers keep their listeners.*

ONE SIMPLE RULE

Here's one simple rule:

- Never tell someone that your problem is worse than theirs. Never. Not ever.

But what happens when you're dying to do just that, to get competitive with another kvetcher? Let's be realistic. We all think our problems are worse than the problems of friends, family members, and coworkers, at least once in a while.

This is perfectly normal. We're only human, when all is said and done. Nothing hurts as much as the shoe that's pinching *your* foot. So what do you do when you can't stand someone's kvetching, when you want more than anything to give them Lewie's line, when you want to say, "You think *you've* got problems!"?

You get a hold of yourself, that's what you do. You take a deep breath and count to ten, and then you resist the temptation to get competitive. This is pure virtue on your part. Praise yourself for doing this. You're practically a saint. But first, leave the scene before temptation overcomes your saintliness. Tell the kvetcher that his problem sounds pretty tough, that you'd love to listen, but you have to leave just now. (This, of course, is true.) Then go and find someone you can kvetch to about your problems. After refraining from competitive kvetching, you need to kvetch. You need to kvetch just to reassure yourself that you still *can*, if for no other reason. Who wants to be a saint? We all know how saints got to be saints. There's just too much suffering in sainthood, at least for me.

THE A.F.O.B. SUPPORT GROUP

My friends have put this principle into action. Two of them, Peter and George, founded what Peter named the A.F.O.B. Support Group. A.F.O.B. stands for Adult Friends of Barbara. When my KPM rate gets too high, they get together to kvetch about my kvetching. That way they can avoid kvetching competitively with me. But they do not become saints. They tell me when the group meets, and then I know I have to turn down my KPMs.

Now I have a confession to make: I'm (secretly) thrilled that my friends have taken my advice. I'm thrilled that they kvetch about me in order to cope with life. I'm thrilled that there are now several A.F.O.B. chapters, including one in Los Angeles. But I'm a little annoyed that in the A.F.O.B. group meetings, my friends support each other—and not me!

CHAPTER 8

STEP 5: IN PRAISE OF KVETCHING

I have some bad news for you, and it's the kind you can't kvetch about. It's not enough to know how to kvetch. It's not enough to know that no problem is too trivial to kvetch about (Step 1). It's not enough to know that you can't kvetch to all of the people all of the time (Step 2), or pretend you aren't kvetching (Step 3), or hog all of the kvetching time (Step 4). You also need to encourage other people to kvetch. This may seem like a moral obligation, but mostly it's a practical necessity. The nature of both the moral obligation and the practical necessity will become clearer as you read this chapter.

Kvetching is a hard sell. Even to kvetchers. Especially to kvetchers. You already know why. Americans don't like to admit that they kvetch—especially when they are kvetching. Even the best kvetchers carry the heavy weight of America's anti-kvetching attitude on their shoulders. So while Americans need to kvetch, like to kvetch, and do kvetch, they don't like to admit it.

This makes teaching Americans to kvetch difficult. It's hard to teach someone a new skill, any new skill. It's even harder to teach a skill that many people don't see as a skill. So if you tell other Americans that you are trying to teach them how to kvetch, you will get resistance. They won't understand why anyone in their right mind would want to learn this. Take my friend Lisa.

A TOUGH CASE

Lisa has an unusually positive attitude toward life. It's even more positive than my friend Andrea's attitude (see Chapter 2). No matter how badly things are going for Lisa, she always says "good" when I ask her how she is. I've known Lisa for years, and she always says she's doing fine, no matter what. This drives me crazy. So I went on a crusade. I decided to teach Lisa to kvetch.

It all began when Lisa broke her finger and went to work anyway. I just happened to drop by Lisa's office to visit her that morning, and I found her sitting at her desk—at her computer!—as if nothing were wrong.

"Hi, Lisa. How goes?"

"Fine." Lisa smiled back at me as always. "And you?"

"I hate everything," I kvetched, "so I guess I'm okay."

Then I noticed Lisa's hand. Her right index finger was swollen; it was at least twice its normal size.

"My God, what's *that*?" I asked, pointing to the oversized finger.

"I think I broke my finger," said Lisa as calmly as ever, and still smiling.

"What?! How can you sit there? How can you *type*? Have you seen a doctor? Have you gone to the emergency room?" I was characteristically upset.

"I didn't want to go to the emergency room yesterday, when I broke it, because this is Maine, where they don't have real emergency rooms. [Notice that in the midst of all this stoicism, there was a hint of kvetching, a glimmer of hope.] I called my doctor and I have an appointment with him for four."

"Four! Lisa, it's nine now—that's seven hours away. You've got to be kidding. What will you do till then?"

"I'll work—at my computer." Lisa was serious. This was a hard case.

"How will you do that with a broken finger?" Maybe the Socratic Method will work, I thought to myself, grasping at straws.

"I just won't use that finger," said Lisa confidently.

"Forget it. I'm taking over." At this point I picked up Lisa's phone and called her doctor, told him the situation, and gave Lisa the plan: "Your doctor says to go to the emergency room. And that's exactly what we're going to do now. This minute. You have no choice."

I drove Lisa to the emergency room, where they X-rayed her finger and pronounced it broken. Emergency called Lisa's doctor, who got Lisa an immediate appointment with an orthopedic surgeon. The orthopedic guy set Lisa's finger. Then I drove Lisa back to her office.

"Why don't you just go home. Surely you can take the day off," I suggested.

"But I have work to do," said Lisa, still smiling.

You see what I was up against? And this wasn't the half of it. I spent years trying to get Lisa to kvetch. Years and years. It drove me crazy. I tried everything I could think of:

- I said "I hate life" (or "I hate everything") at least twice a week.

- I pointed out things in life we all are entitled to kvetch about (like having a broken finger).

- I explained how being too cheerful can be bad for you.

- I noticed every quasi-kvetch that Lisa uttered, and I tried to help her turn it into something more substantial.

Nothing worked. Nothing. No matter what, Lisa just smiled. She smiled and smiled, while I kvetched and kvetched. Lisa was my toughest case ever.

In Praise of Kvetching

And then, one day, Lisa started kvetching. Not the kind of hard-core kvetching you get from a pro like me. Just her own quiet, modest, low-key style of kvetching. But it was real kvetching, and it occurred on a regular basis. Yikes, I thought. Was it there all along and I had simply missed it? After all, Lisa did kvetch about emergency rooms in Maine the day she broke her finger. Was I looking for *my* style of kvetching and failing to notice *her* style? Thinking back over the years, I recalled that Lisa did send me distress signals when something was wrong, and that if I asked her about the signal, she would tell me the problem. Was she actually kvetching back then? I couldn't think of the answer. I couldn't resolve the question with mere armchair speculation. So I did the practical thing. I went straight to the horse's mouth. I asked Lisa what happened. Had she been kvetching all along, or had she changed?

WHAT MADE THE DIFFERENCE?

Lisa said she had changed. She now felt freer to kvetch, but she wasn't sure what had made the difference. She said it might have been watching me kvetch that did it. Of course, she couldn't be sure about that. But Lisa said she was certain about how she got to be kvetching-challenged in the first place. She said she was raised to be happy and smile no matter what. She was raised to think that everything was fine the way it was—or at least to *say* everything was fine—

no matter how bad things got. So Lisa felt wrong or bad—she felt guilty—if she didn't act happy all of the time. Lisa says that watching me kvetch may have helped her feel more okay about giving up her nonstop smiling, giving up the pretense. She says that watching me kvetch may have helped her feel more okay about doing some kvetching of her own. As Lisa says, we can't be sure that my kvetching is what did the trick—but it's nice to think that Lisa wanted to give me some of the credit.

To me, it sounded as if Lisa was indeed raised with the all-American anti-kvetching attitude. Lisa really was kvetching-challenged—a condition surely caused, at least in part, by her keep-smiling-no-matter-what background. She may also lack the "kvetching gene." But since we know little about the biology of kvetching, I am not so sure about that. In any case, the good news is that Lisa learned to kvetch. She learned to kvetch despite having these American obstacles to kvetching. This encourages me—a lot. That's because Lisa has been my toughest case so far. If she can learn to kvetch, *anyone* can. And if there's any truth in Lisa's own idea about what helped her to start kvetching, then having a good strong role model is all the more important. So one way to teach people how to kvetch is to be a kvetcher yourself, to be a role model for kvetching. But be a role model for creative kvetching.

As important as having kvetchy role models can be, I think something else helped Lisa; something else made the difference. It is this: I stopped using many of the tactics in my list just above. Of course, I kept telling Lisa "I hate life"—that's my trademark. I kept kvetching about my own life. I kept being a role model. But I stopped pointing out how hard life is, how being too cheerful can be bad for you, and so on. In short, I stopped doing what wasn't working. Giving up on strategies that don't work is a well-kept secret. Few people ever figure out that if your so-called "solution" to a problem doesn't work, you should stop using it. Stop using the old, ineffective solution, and do something different. Not just any old "something different" will always work, but anything different is bound to be better than "the same old thing."

I should have known this from the start. The idea is ancient, but it was popularized in the 1970s and 1980s by what therapists called strategic therapy. Therapists who learned about strategic therapy stuck to one motto: When you've got a thorny problem, stop doing "more of the same" and try something different. That's what I did with Lisa.

What did I do that was different? I cut out the old ways of trying to get Lisa to kvetch. Instead, I just praised her whenever she did kvetch. I listened carefully to Lisa, and whenever I heard her kvetch, I praised her kvetching. Even the slightest kvetch brought words of praise to my lips. Nothing fancy. Just something like, "Lisa, you kvetched. Good for you!" And then I let it go at that. No suggesting that she try to kvetch more substantially. No lectures about the virtues of kvetching. Just plain old praise. Pure and simple. And sure enough, little by little, Lisa started to kvetch. In her own quiet way, of course: No fanfare, no ranting, no raving. Nothing fancy, nothing profound. Just her own quiet version of kvetching. But it was kvetching nonetheless. And so Lisa kvetched about the cost of day care, her shinsplints, how there was never enough time to get everything done. She kvetched about being stuck in a cold climate, about missing life in the city, about how much her finger still hurt her— even years later. So you see, even the toughest cases, even the most kvetching-challenged Americans, have some kvetching in them. You just have to know where to look. You just have to find it, and then praise it.

I knew we were home free when Lisa told me she was working on becoming a kvetcher. It was a thrilling moment. I had helped create another kvetcher. I had helped make America a better place.

HOW TO GET PEOPLE TO KVETCH

When dealing with the kvetching-challenged (most Americans, that is), you must be patient. But not infinitely patient. Learn from my experience with Lisa. Follow these simple steps.

- Look for any sign of kvetching you can detect in a person who is kvetching-challenged.

In Praise of Kvetching

See if you can notice kvetching whenever and wherever it occurs. Before you try to increase it, you must detect it. It may be all around you. But you may be trained to ignore it. Or it may not take the form your own kvetching takes. Be on the lookout.

• When you find a sign of kvetching, praise it.

Don't make a big deal. Just say something like, "You know, that was pretty good kvetching." Or, "Good for you, you kvetched! Most Americans can't do that." You can use the word "complain" instead of "kvetch," but then you lose the opportunity to teach your "student" about kvetching proper. Besides, you will be more intriguing if you praise someone for something they've never heard of.

There are sound psychological principles to support this step. They come from what psychologists call learning theory. That's the psychological term for something you already know. You already know that if you want to increase a certain behavior, you need to reward it. Remember when you got gold stars from your teacher for behaving yourself? If you liked getting gold stars, or if you liked your teacher's approval, you probably kept on behaving yourself. The same idea works with praise. If your praise means something to someone else, it can change the way they behave.

Start by praising any sign of kvetching, no matter how small it may be. First things first: Any step in the right direction is a good step. For example, if you ask someone how he is, and instead of the usual "fine" he says "just fair," congratulate him for not saying "fine." Then, once that person actually starts to kvetch, you can refine his technique. You can help him to kvetch more creatively. How? By praising kvetching that gets closer to creative kvetching. This is called response shaping in learning theory. You get more precise about the kind of behavior you praise. So at first you praise any sign of kvetching; later on you praise only good solid kvetching; and finally you praise only good solid creative kvetching.

- Be a role model: Kvetch!

It's not enough to praise others. You must show people what you want them to learn. You must be a good role model. You must kvetch. But you must kvetch creatively. If you kvetch creatively, you will attract people with your kvetching, even people who are kvetching-challenged. Then they will see the benefits of kvetching. Then they will be motivated to kvetch. People learn best when they are motivated to learn.

ABOUT YOUR MORAL OBLIGATION: THE SELF-SACRIFICE

Okay, I confess. My 5-step program is like some 12-

step recovery programs in this one way (and only in this one way): Like them, I tell you that once you have achieved your goal, you must "give something back." Once you have learned to kvetch, you must teach others to kvetch. It's a moral obligation. It's not the usual moral obligation, though; in fact, it's a rather unusual moral obligation. But it's a moral obligation nonetheless.

What is the nature of that moral obligation? Since my program is not a recovery program, you are not helping others to recover from a disease of any sort. So in that way, my final step is not like the final step of many 12-step programs. You are not saving individual souls. You are not saving bodies and minds—not your own, not anyone else's. So breathe a sigh of relief. You are not here to help heal.

What you are doing is this: You are helping American Culture. You are helping America get past its anti-kvetching attitude. You are helping America overcome the History, Psychology, Psychotherapy, Self-Help, and Biology that contribute to America's anti-kvetching attitude. By teaching Americans to kvetch, you are making America a better place. A place where kvetchers can live with freedom and dignity. Where kvetchers can hold their heads high. Where all Americans can be free to stop smiling and start kvetching, if they want to.

WHY THE MORAL OBLIGATION IS NOT SELFLESS: THE PRACTICAL NECESSITY

If you have read this book, you know why your moral obligation is a perfectly selfish one. You know why, in the end, it's in your own interest as a kvetcher to teach others to kvetch—to kvetch creatively, that is.

Have you figured out why this is so? The answer is simple: Teaching people to kvetch creatively puts more creative kvetchers in America. The more creative kvetchers there are out there, the more listeners there are on hand for your own kvetching. It's hard to kvetch to people who are kvetching-challenged, or people who are themselves noncreative kvetchers. The kvetching-challenged types tell you to cheer up; the noncreative kvetchers get competitive with you. Neither will do when you want someone to listen attentively to your own kvetching.

THE ORDER OF KVETCHERS

To keep kvetching creatively, remember this:

- Teach others to kvetch so that you can keep on kvetching.

The induction of novices into the Order of Kvetchers ensures a lifetime supply of listeners who can tolerate your own kvetching. If you teach them well, they may even appreciate your own kvetching. This is why you must become a "missionary." This is why you must teach others the fine art of creative kvetching.

KEEP SMILING, KEEP KVETCHING

Americans like to smile a lot. Whether it's cultural or biological, they can't help it. They can't stop smiling—no matter what. Lisa is like that. She now kvetches, but she still smiles a lot. My friend Kate does the same thing. She has learned to kvetch, but she hasn't learned to stop smiling.

This combination of smiling and kvetching used to bother me. The question is, Can someone really kvetch if they smile while they are kvetching? I used to think not, but now I'm not so sure. So I asked Kate about it.

Kate said she sees no problem, no contradiction. She says it's okay to smile a lot as long as deep down inside you know that life is really hard. It's okay to smile as long as you admit to yourself and others that sometimes you're pretty miserable. As long as you know how to kvetch. As long as you actually do kvetch.

So here is the rule for those of you who can't stop smiling:

• You can keep smiling, as long as you keep kvetching.

PART III

GOOD AND BAD ROLE MODELS

CHAPTER 9

FAMOUS CREATIVE
AND NONCREATIVE KVETCHERS

My husband David and I have a friend, Wes, who recently moved to a retirement community.

I'm no expert on retirement communities, but I can tell you this much: I've visited quite a few retirement communities, and there's a whole lot of kvetching going on in those places. And why shouldn't there be? These are *retirement* communities, after all. Let's face it, aging is no picnic; aging gives you *lots* to kvetch about.

I've been to Wes's retirement community several times now. Often enough to get the distinct impression that most—or at least many—of the residents there have never even heard (let alone uttered) the word "kvetch." In other words, it's a pretty WASPy place. So it's probably safe to say that most of the residents don't have the "kvetching gene." I've also gotten the impression that most of the residents would, if asked, say that kvetching is not a good thing. This means that most of them probably have an anti-kvetching attitude. Yet they kvetch. They may not call it kvetching, but still they kvetch. I myself have heard them kvetch—this is no mere conjecture on my part. But this also presents a problem: If you have an anti-kvetching attitude (whatever its cause), and if you kvetch anyway, you are bound to deny your own kvetching. So even though the average age in Wes's retirement community is eightysomething, I bet most of the kvetchers there are KIDs (Kvetchers in Denial). One never knows for sure, so with the help of my husband David, I did some checking.

Last week, David visited Wes at his retirement community. Seated around a large table were David, Wes, and two female residents of the community: Grace, a stately woman in her mid-eighties, and Betsy, a mere child of seventy-seven. According to David, the conversation turned to the problem of complaining—how lots of residents in the retirement community complained a great deal. (I wasn't there, but it sounded to me as if Wes, Grace, and Betsy were upset about all the kvetching going on—a sure sign of an anti-kvetching attitude.) David decided to take the opportunity to discuss my "kvetching" book, as he called it. He wanted to introduce the word "kvetch," and see how my ideas about kvetching played out in that setting.

"My wife's writing a book about complaining," David said. "Actually, it's a book about kvetching."

"What's kvetching?" the two women asked. Wes didn't have to ask. He's known me for quite a few years.

"It's Yiddish for complaining." David obviously didn't want to recite all of Chapter 1. "But what's most important about my wife's book is her distinction between creative kvetching and noncreative kvetching." David said he went on to explain the distinction, and that his lunch companions seemed more than a little interested.

"That book would certainly sell here!" Grace said. "It would be very helpful. Here, just about everyone complains, but few will admit it. I certainly would buy it."

When David told me this, I thought to myself that if octogenarians (who may be KIDs) can be convinced of the value of kvetching, so can the rest of America. There's hope for us yet.

KNOW YOUR CREATIVE AND NONCREATIVE KVETCHERS

Wes says he finds the distinction between creative kvetching and noncreative kvetching quite useful. He says he has tried to sort out (in his own mind) those who are creative kvetchers, and those who are noncreative kvetchers. He won't tell me who, in his opinion, fits into each category. But he does tell me that the distinction between creative and noncreative kvetching has helped him understand his reactions to different people. This is a good thing. I'm glad to know that my distinction can produce this kind of self-awareness. Who knows? Maybe Wes will follow the five steps, especially Step 5, and increase the rate of creative kvetching in his retirement community. If everyone did this, the world would be a better place. But what really impresses me is Wes's interest in kvetching. If someone like Wes, who probably lacks the "kvetching gene," can see the merits of creative kvetching, there's hope for the rest of us.

We could all benefit from Wes's mental exercise. But how would we know if we had classified our targets correctly? How would we know that we had correctly identified the creative kvetchers and the noncreative kvetchers? We'd have to discuss our decisions with people who knew each other well. Then there would be a whole lot of hurt feelings. That's because everyone would know who got labeled a noncreative kvetcher. Even those who got called a creative kvetcher might be upset by the idea that they are seen as kvetching at all. And before the exercise was over, no one would be talking to anyone else. No, this exercise is too risky. It's not a good way to test your appreciation of the distinction between creative and noncreative kvetching. It's not a good way to choose your kvetchy role models.

But we could consider famous people—people most of us have watched on TV or on film. They can serve as our examples of creative and noncreative kvetchers. So I brainstormed with some of my friends, and we came up with our own little list.

FAMOUS KVETCHERS

THE DOOM CHANNEL

MANKOFF

"Bad things are happening.   *"Worse to come.*
Real bad."   *Much worse."*

FAMOUS CREATIVE KVETCHERS

The famous creative kvetchers, like all creative kvetchers, draw us in with their kvetching. We find their kvetching to be fun and entertaining, sometimes even witty and true. They instinctively follow my five steps. That's part of the reason for their fame. (Although, to be fair, many famous people are famous for reasons other than their kvetching style—for example, Vincent Van Gogh probably didn't kvetch enough, but he's famous nonetheless.) In fact, I think many famous people are famous precisely because they kvetch creatively. They're famous because they express the difficulties of life for us in ways that draw us in. For those of us who are kvetching-challenged, we can kvetch vicariously through the famous creative kvetchers. We can also follow their example when we learn to do our own kvetching.

1. Princess Diana

Diana was at the top of my list. And with good reason. If nothing else, the reaction in England to her death makes the case—Diana literally taught the Brits how to kvetch. The subtitle of a *New Yorker* magazine piece (September 15, 1997) says it all: "Farewell to Diana, and to Britain's stiff upper lip."

Incidentally, **Fergie** must have been taking notes. Her kvetching style is more self-deprecating—have you seen her Weight Watchers commercials on TV? She does what I call "comedic kvetching," but she's got the five steps down pat. Who knows, maybe the Brit stiff upper lip is now a thing of the past. Maybe the Brits are finally ready to admit that they know full well how to kvetch, that they have been kvetching their hearts out for centuries. Maybe they will stop being KIDs, and become creative kvetchers.

2. Murphy Brown

Fortunately for me, I'm not **Dan Quayle** (who is not a creative kvetcher). So, unlike him, I know that Murphy Brown (played by **Candice Bergen** on TV) is a *fictional* character. But she's a great creative kvetcher, and because she's on TV, we can watch her to see just how she does it.

Murphy is brash, outspoken, abrasive, and obnoxious. Her coworkers want to kill her, but underneath it all they love her. And we love to watch her. Why? Because she kvetches creatively. She knows when to kvetch and when to shut up and listen. She never—well, almost never—pretends she's not kvetching when she is kvetching. She doesn't try kvetching to all of the people all of the time—she knows there's no point in kvetching to her countless secretaries. She knows when to kvetch, like all great comedic kvetchers.

143

We could all learn a great deal about the fine art of creative kvetching by watching Murphy—even if only in syndication.

3. Most Comedians

Have you ever noticed that most comedians are really expert kvetchers? Think about it. Most comedians kvetch about *something*—themselves, their parents, their spouses, school, politicians, love, sex, whatever, as long as it's good kvetching material. That's because good comedy is often good social criticism. It ridicules what's wrong with us, with our society—with life itself. To do that and get laughs, you have to kvetch creatively. Otherwise, who'd want to listen? Good comedians know how to raise our collective kvetch reception potential.

Rodney Dangerfield is one of the best kvetchy comedians. His act is based on one kvetchy complaint: That he "gets no respect." **Murphy Brown** has some of that element too—not getting any respect—in her kvetching. **David Letterman** kvetches in a hostile way, and **Jay Leno** kvetches in a friendly way, but they both kvetch. **Bob Newhart** and **Brett Butler** kvetch in WASPy ways, while **Woody Allen**, **Elaine Boosler**, and **Joan Rivers** kvetch in nonWASPy ways. But they all kvetch. When Joan Rivers says, "Can we talk?," you know she's going to kvetch about something.

And if you think about it, in most sitcoms the characters spend their time kvetching about how lousy their lives are going. Think about **George** and **Elaine** in **Jerry Seinfeld's** show. *Seinfeld* was said to be a show about nothing, but my friend Mikey says it was *really* all about kvetching. Mikey says **Newman** was the only character on the show who never kvetched—and he was the evil one. Think about **Chandler, Ross,** and **Rachel** in the sitcom *Friends*. Think about **Cybill** and **Maryann** in **Cybill Shepherd's** show. Even **Lucy Ricardo**, whose comedy was largely physical, kvetched lots in every episode of *I Love Lucy*. The characters who have a positive attitude, like **Phoebe** in *Friends*, are funny precisely because they *aren't* kvetching—they're the foils for the kvetchers.

4. Country/Folk/Rock/Pop Singers

Consider the lyrics of pop music. There's a whole lot of kvetching going on out there. Country takes the cake—it's always been about unrequited love, or worse: Remember **Tammy Wynette's** big hit "D-I-V-O-R-C-E"? Folk music has always had kvetchy themes: Remember the protest songs of the sixties? **Bob Dylan** and **Leonard Cohen** did some great musical kvetching. They still do. (So does **Joan Baez.**) Hard rock has had its kvetchy moments: Remember **Janis Joplin's** "Lord, Won't You Buy Me a Mercedes Benz"

145

and **Mick Jagger's** recording of "I Can't Get No Satisfaction"? And we shouldn't leave out the more recently popular punk and rap music: Consider **Ice T's** lyrics, for example.

5. All Consumer Advocates

Ralph Nader. Need I say more?

6. Philosophers

Kierkegaard, Nietzsche, and **Schopenhauer,** to name just a few.

FAMOUS NONCREATIVE KVETCHERS

The famous noncreative kvetchers drive us away with their kvetching. We find their kvetching to be sour and excessive (not that they notice), filled with self-pity and competitiveness. They ignore the five steps. Still, we must identify a few of them too, because there are lessons to be learned from both types of kvetchers.

But first, think about this: To be a *famous* noncreative kvetcher, you have to draw in enough people to be famous. You at least have to attract attention. That takes a certain amount of creativity in itself. So it's hard to find good examples of *famous* noncreative kvetching. Unless you turn to politicians, which I do. My friends and I put our heads together again, and here's what we came up with.

1. Newt Gingrich

Newt worked hard on becoming America's most famous noncreative kvetcher. He realized his dream—to be Speaker of the House. And then what did he do? He spent all his time kvetching noncreatively. Remember all that kvetching about how he didn't get to sit up front with the President in Air Force One? A legitimate complaint—as all complaints are. So Newt seemed to understand Step 1—Our Inalienable Right to Kvetch.

Newt's problem was that he didn't follow the other four steps to creative kvetching. Newt tried to kvetch to all of the people all of the time—even after he *won*. So he ignored Step 2. He pretended he wasn't kvetching when he was. So he ignored Step 3. And Newt was a real competitive kvetcher—he made it sound like *his* problems (for example, with the press), were worse than anyone else's. So he flunked Step 4. And as for Step 5, well, I have never heard Newt sing the praises of kvetching. Have you? Here's a thought: Could it be that Newt was forced to resign precisely because he was such a noncreative kvetcher?

Bob Dole gets an honorary mention as a noncreative kvetcher. But then he lost the presidential election and started making fun of himself. If he's not careful, he could become a creative kvetcher. Then he might win another election. I'm tempted to give **Ross Perot** an honorary mention, too. But it's hard to call him a kvetcher of any sort, since no one can quite figure out just what he's talking about, or doing.

2. Charlie Brown

Like **Murphy Brown, Charlie Brown,** of the "Peanuts" cartoon, is a fictional character. And even though *we* love him (no doubt because we identify with his pain about the harshness of life), the "Peanuts" kids have real problems with him. They're not sure how to play with him. They're not sure what to say to him. That's because Charlie is a noncreative kvetcher. So he always ends up alone, and then he kvetches about it, and then he ends up more alone. Even his dog **Snoopy** gets sick of listening to Charlie's problems.

In fairness to Charlie, he has sought help—he pays **Lucy** five cents for psychiatric sessions. But Lucy's "help" never helps Charlie. And the reason for that is obvious: Lucy tells Charlie to stop complaining and start smiling. She tells him to stop making mountains out of molehills, to cheer up, to look on the bright side, to get involved.

Of course, we know that Lucy is giving Charlie all the wrong advice. Charlie needs advice about how to kvetch creatively. Snoopy knows how to do that. **Woodstock** loves to hang out with Snoopy, even when Snoopy is kvetching. Snoopy should teach Charlie how to kvetch creatively.

3. Sports Figures

Sports figures have a big burden to carry. We want—
no, we expect—our athletes to be good sports. We expect
them to be cheerful no matter what. So *any* kvetching they
do is automatically unbecoming. Any kvetching they do is
automatically noncreative. Remember **Tonya Harding**?
She's the figure skater who was mixed up with the guy who
injured the leg of her figure-skating rival, **Nancy Kerrigan**.
For a while Tonya kvetched, and lots of sports fans never
took her seriously again. Nancy kvetched too, and fans found
it unbecoming. The great tennis star **John McEnroe** used to
yell at the linesmen. For some it was entertaining. But after
a while, many fans were not amused. Would he have been
better off kvetching about the linesmen instead of yelling at
them? I think so. In any case, John cleaned up his act. Then
all was forgiven.

Then there's all of **American baseball**. Remember the
baseball strike? It was one very long stretch of kvetching. It
took Americans quite a while to recover from that. After all,
baseball is America's game. How can America's game be
reduced to a kvetching fest? The real problem was that there
was nothing creative about it. Nothing.

A FINAL WORD

You can be a creative kvetcher. Unless you are a professional athlete, you can learn to kvetch creatively. Just follow the five simple steps to creative kvetching. Your life won't be all okay, but at least you'll have one problem under control. Of course, there will still be lots to worry about, lots to kvetch about. Remember, life is hard—always.

And remember my Achilles tendons. I have to admit that they're getting better. But they still bother me much of the time.

151

AUDENREED PRESS

ORDER FORM

Please send

_____ copies of
Stop Smiling, Start Kvetching @ $9.95   _____

Sales Tax, Maine only, add 5.5% ($ .56 per copy)   _____

Shipping: $2.00 first book
                 $ .50 each additional book
Priority
Shipping: $4.00 first book   _____

                                                    TOTAL   _____

Send check or money order to:

Audenreed Press
PMB 103
P.O. Box 1305
Brunswick, Maine 04011
(207) 833-5016

Or call (for orders only):
        1-888-315-0582
Internet orders:
        www.biddle-audenreed.com

NAME   _____

ADDRESS   _____

                     _____

                     _____

PHONE   _____

AUDENREED PRESS   ORDER FORM

Please send

_____ copies of
Stop Smiling, Start Kvetching @ $9.95   _____

Sales Tax, Maine only, add 5.5% ($ .56 per copy)   _____

Shipping: $2.00 first book
           $ .50 each additional book
Priority
Shipping: $4.00 first book   _____

                              TOTAL   _____

Send check or money order to:

Audenreed Press
PMB 103
P.O. Box 1305
Brunswick, Maine 04011
(207) 833-5016

Or call (for orders only):
        1-888-315-0582
Internet orders:
        www.biddle-audenreed.com

NAME   _____

ADDRESS   _____

            _____

            _____

PHONE   _____

Critical Acclaim for
STOP SMILING, START KVETCHING

"In *Stop Smiling, Start Kvetching: A 5-Step Guide to Creative Complaining*, Barbara Held's genuine humor with a practical and unique approach to self-help is based on the premise that having to act happy (or worse, actually be happy) when the harsh realities of life descend upon us is to add insult to injury. Rather, the trick to true happiness under trying circumstances is to know how to complain (kvetch) properly, so that we attract others, including their assistance and resources, rather than repel them. . . . *Stop Smiling, Start Kvetching* is the ideal antidote to all those other saccharine and submissive self-help books."

Michael J. Carson—*Midwest Book Review*

"The author contends that other self-help books with their message that you have to act happy and be happy all the time are often just a guilt trip that ignores the fact that we often encounter things worth complaining about. She does so with refreshing humor and I think this book will prove helpful to those too timid to complain when they should."

Alan Caruba—*Bookviews*

"Help has arrived for the chronically cheerful. Buy and read Barbara's book; even if you only like some of it, you will learn how to complain about the other parts."

Frederick Crews
Author, *The Pooh Perplex*